Praise for

DON'T DO ANYTHING STUPID

I am glad my friend John chose to write a book on racism. His book has many great points and is a magnificent guide for those who are committed to personal growth in the area of race relations.

—Dr. Kelvin Croom, Senior Pastor, College Hill Baptist Church

This book is amazing; absolutely amazing. I think John was led by the Holy Spirit on this project and I hope great things come from it. I see the ability to gain insight and understanding and empathy as major possibilities for those who take the time to read and reflect.

—Robert Harris, Director of Diversity and Inclusion, BancorpSouth

This book is a wonderful primer for anyone who wants to start the conversation about race in America without feeling like they are walking on crushed glass. One powerful point of the book is John offers solutions to explore. We have to start somewhere, and John provides a good start.

—Debra Stokes, Christian Life Coach, Civic Leader, and Author

This book is like chipping paint—it's messy but it needs to be done or nothing new will stick. If I had my druthers, I would put this book on every white man's mandatory reading list. This book has expanded my perspectives, and I admit to trying to convince myself that I was above the fray.

—Bob Elder, Retired US Navy Captain

God really used John in writing this piece of work. He would never have been able to finish it in such a short time span had the Holy Spirit not been guiding the way. I think the impact it will have is to help us all start to heal.

—Kerry Stevenson, Assistant Football Coach, The University of Tennessee

John's book is extremely thought-provoking while at the same time an interesting and easy read. This book is very timely and a topic all races need to discuss, if we as a nation are to get any further down the road to better understanding each other.

—Bruce Hedrick, former General Manager, Chinese-American Joint Venture

For those of us that are leaders, finding a way to discuss the important topic of racism is a difficult task. In this book, John gives us a language to discuss racism without the hyperbole and extremes so often used today. Checking our assumptions, and remembering that our life experiences are not necessarily normal for others, are both powerful steps forward. Embracing our differences rather than denying them will help move us toward a more productive relationship with our brothers and sisters of different racial backgrounds. Read this book through a lens of love and acceptance for all persons. Thank you, John, for helping us navigate these troubled waters.

—Rev. James Farmer, retired

Don't Do Anything Stupid is full of empathy for black as well as white folks. That plus the simplicity and softness of John's writing style makes the book very effective. This book reminds me of a Hindi poem that loosely translates as, "Imparting wisdom is like knocking on a door. The object is not to break it open but to get it open."

—Sanjeev Gupta, CEO and Founder of Realization, INC

John Covington is always thinking. In today's world that is not a common trait. He thinks about service. He thinks about production flows and constraints to making things work better. He thinks about training dogs. He thinks about leadership. He thinks about how all of these things might connect in some way. Now he is thinking about how we should interact with others, especially those who might be a different color than we are, or who grew up in a different culture than we did. John's writings are always worth reading!

—Tom Kilgore, CEO TVA, retired

I have followed John for decades. Each of his books, blogs, and presentations are unique in that they always bring wisdom. This book takes it to a whole new level. Not only does it dive deeply into a burning topic, but it does so from a unique perspective. He does so openly, with humility and love for others. This is his best work yet!

—Brad Newman, Plant Manager, ZF Group

John Covington shares a lifetime of personal experiences and anecdotes about race relations in his very readable book. The reader will find many thought-provoking questions which are excellent conversation starters for church groups and book clubs.

—Byron P. Brought, Minister of Congregational Care, Severna Park United Methodist Church

DON'T DO ANYTHING STUPID

A White Man's Guide to Racial Harmony

JOHN COVINGTON

CALLED WRITERS
CHRISTIAN PUBLISHING

Copyright

Contents

Foreword

The inevitable comfort zone. How many times in your life have you been prodded with the best of intentions to get out of your comfort zone? In his seventh book on leadership and faith, John Covington tackles the always sensitive topic of racism. But he does so with a message of heartfelt intentionality aimed at those of us he can influence the most—white males.

Don't Do Anything Stupid is a casual, somewhat comical, and realistic look at our own innate biases, whether recognized or not, and the silly things we sometimes do to declare our innocence toward racism. John weaves his charming anecdotal stories into a collective narrative that helps you understand how simple it is to find common ground with individuals of other races. Although you may not agree with every perspective he offers, you will come away knowing his heart is in the right place.

To know John is to observe and admire his dedication

toward a multitude of civic interests. I personally know him through a student and civic leadership advisory board he and I have had the pleasure to serve. He is always gracious with his time, measured in his response, and genuinely happy to be among people from all walks of life. His decision to write about racism couldn't have been easy. But the candor with which he writes puts the reader at ease, free of any worries that he might have a hidden agenda.

As a former University of Alabama National Alumni Association president, I have been confronted with the systemic racism John highlights. For me, it was demonstrated by the lack of minority regional and district vice-presidents on our Executive Committee. We were told the black community had little interest in being involved. Perhaps that was true in times past—I cannot say. But I can confirm that as of today, the UA Black Alumni Association is an official chapter of the UA National Alumni Association. Let's call it progress with a dose of intentionality behind it.

Read the book and be inspired by how many of John's illustrations have been true in your own life.

L. Alex Smith
Past President 2016-17
National Alumni Association
The University of Alabama

Introduction

"If you could snap your fingers and make it happen, what would you want white men to understand about racism?"

That's a question I asked several of my black friends. Their answers were among several factors that motivated me to write this book. My heart breaks for the black men and women in my life. They are my friends and loved ones and when they hurt, so do I. These are issues of right and wrong—justice and injustice.

As a white male, I know in my heart that I must do whatever I can to help.

Here are some of my friends' answers:

- *For them to just realize it exists. Most white people do not think racism exists today.*

- *White people like to say, "I cannot be a racist; I have five black friends." They see good blacks and bad blacks. The good blacks are their five friends; the bad blacks are all the rest of the black people.*

- *My 17-year-old son wanted to go out on Halloween with his white buddies. I told him no, he could not go. I was afraid if they did some mischief and he was running away, he would be shot. When he goes out at night, I do not worry about him being in an accident, I worry about him being pulled over by the police.*

- *The KKK marched in our Christmas parade and showed up at my youth football games. I have been pulled over by the police for no reason and followed. I graduated from high school in 1997.*

- *Empathy is the key to all of this—the ability to imagine one's self in another's place and then asking the questions: Is this okay? Is this acceptable? And if the answer is no, then have the courage to change it.*

- *To recognize that privilege and bias does exist in society. It is not the fault of all whites that*

*privilege exists. It's systemic and it has
festered in the fabric of our society for decades.*

- *To realize there can be two different
  experiences for whites and blacks in many
  different situations.*

- *Many of your black employees are exhausted,
  scared, crying in between meetings, putting on
  a performance, and mentally checking out.*

- *The work to end racism in America is not
  someone else's problem. It is an American
  problem and to address it is just as patriotic as
  the flag is red, white, and blue.*

My friends, this book openly discusses racism. I am
primarily addressing relations between white people and
black people in the United States. I've chosen to use
those terms—white and black—for race because in my
experience, those are the terms most often used by people
in everyday life.

The purpose of this book is not to outline a
systematic plan for eradicating racism from our society.
Rather, the purpose of the book is to encourage us to
think—to reflect more deeply on the issue of racism. I
hope to inspire all of us to examine ourselves and then
actively work on our own hearts. My ultimate aim is to
get us all thinking about how we can do more in our daily

lives to help address the problem of racism—step by step, little by little.

Much of what I say will be universal truths that can apply across various races and locations, but other parts of the book may not apply as directly. And while other people may have interest in reading this book, the primary audience I'm targeting is white men. So please allow me to address white men directly for a moment here in the introduction.

If you are like me, you have used the phrase "I am color blind" when referring to your approach toward racism. Please join with me to stop saying that, because you and I both know it isn't true. Race matters. Color matters. Gender matters. Age matters. All of these things matter, and we know they do. They are part of who God made us to be.

"Before I made you in your mother's womb, I chose you. Before you were born, I set you apart for a special work." (Jeremiah 1:5 ICB)

All of us are unique. We have our own special identity. Part of that identity is race, color, gender, age, and a multitude of other things. Maybe you are a veteran, a musician, an athlete—all part of the package that makes up your identity.

So we all have multiple factors that make up our identity, but we typically only select a few to build our self-identity, meaning *how we see ourselves*. This self-view can change depending on our situation. If I am at a gathering of chemical engineers, then my identity as a chemical engineer oozes up to the surface. Later that day, when I go to a church meeting about prison ministry, my identity as a chemical engineer slips down on the list. My identity as a member of my church goes up a few notches.

Outside of any specific context, when I consider who I am on the whole, being white is way down on the totem pole. My gut feel is that this is the same for most white men. Yes, I am a white male, but that's not something I often consider. Is it different for people of other races? If so, do we need to consider this in our relationships with people of other races?

My wife, Linda, asked me why I was writing this book. "Because I think God told me to and I want to be obedient." Linda thinks I am crazy. However, I choose not to self-identify as crazy.

If I had to guess why God chose me to write this book, I would say it was due to my perspective—which might be somewhat unique to discussions of race taking place in this country. Most of the books I have seen on racism are written by liberals, women, pastors, or academics. Does the ordinary white male relate to their perspectives? Do terms like *white privilege*, *white supremacy*, and *institutional racism* resonate with the average white male? Probably not. In fact, those terms probably do more to alienate the average white male, pushing us further back into a shell of silence and inaction.

That's not what any of us should want. Instead, our goal should be to work together to end racism in all its forms. If each of us can increase our awareness concerning racism and take some concrete action steps, we can begin to truly deal with injustice. This will lead to a more equitable, peaceful, and loving society—and that's something we all should want.

ONE

Albert

"Something here is wrong. I know you do not understand. Perhaps one day you will. Maybe you will even try to bring some justice and make a difference. You seem like a nice kid. Do you know that just pausing a second to gaze into your eyes in a loving manner could bring me harm? No, you don't. However, your mom also seems nice and I doubt she would bring harm to me—I don't think. Farewell young man, whatever your name is. If we meet again, it will be on the other side. Bless you." - Albert

Albert was a thin black man, about 45 years old. He was dressed in a white dress shirt, blue dress slacks, and black shoes. He was of medium height, and I can recall him bending over slightly to look into my eyes. Although he had a somber and melancholy demeanor, I was not afraid. I remember that I liked him. Later on though, I did learn that something was wrong—very wrong.

It was around 1955 in Oakton, Virginia. Oakton is located in the northern part of Virginia, and at the time, it was only a small rural community. Oakton was named for an enormous oak tree that once stood tall in the heart of this little town. Though not without its flaws, Oakton was a picturesque environment for a little boy to grow up in, learn about life, and explore the world around him. There were quaint neighborhoods with plenty of other kids, a source of constant companionship. Nearby there were woods to play in, creeks to cross, and a great deal of trees to climb.

There was just one problem. Until I met Albert, I had never seen a black person before. I was seven years old, and he was the first black person I had ever laid eyes on. What happened that day has bugged me on and off for about the last three decades.

Later on in the day, I asked my mother why all those black people were coming to our house. All I know is that it had something to do with registering to vote. The details are unclear, but I know that my mom was getting paid, apparently to administer some kind of test.

My best guess is that Albert did not pass the test, and therefore was not allowed to vote. However, he did cast a lasting vote with me.

As I write this, the date is May 20th, 2020, putting my encounter with Albert around 65 years in the past. Yet, that day still comes to my mind every so often, much more so in the recent past. Around two weeks ago during my morning prayer time, God hinted that he wanted me to write a book on racism. I thought, "Seriously, God?

You know I'm an old white guy who lives in Alabama, right? You must be thinking of someone else."

When it became clear that he wasn't mistaken, nor was he joking, I realized I was going to need a lot of help. At that point, I began to ask the Lord to help me understand my experience with Albert. Was it a divine appointment? What was the purpose? Why does it still come back to my mind, all these years later?

As I pondered those questions, I decided to go out for my morning walk. Willow and I go for a walk most every morning, much of which is on the Tall Pines Golf Course in Tuscaloosa, Alabama. Willow is my two-year-old German shepherd. While on the golf course, I sometimes let her off the leash. She's always incredibly grateful as this gives her the opportunity to chase geese, eat goose poop, and be on the lookout for one of her many canine pals to play and romp around with.

During this time, we were well into the initial stages of the Coronavirus Pandemic. It had been a stressful time, but also a time to deepen one's faith and become closer to God. The Bible teaches that if we move closer to God, he will move closer to us. One common effect of getting closer to God is that he may ask you to do something, or as my pastor likes to say, "You might *get to* do something."

"So I get to write a book about racism?" I thought to myself, while walking Willow and continuing to ponder my experience with Albert.

It was a beautiful morning. I've never seen an ugly golf course, and at 6:30 in the morning, there are no golfers. It's a wonderful forum for God to reveal important truths and impart his wisdom to me. As Willow was busy sniffing around for goose poop, I soaked in the beauty of the nature surrounding me—a pond, a stream, green grass, tall trees, and birds of all kinds. That particular day, God used my morning walk to reveal an important truth about issues of race.

Though I now work as a business consultant, I am an engineer by training and education. So I do a lot of geeky stuff in my daily life. For example, with my morning walk, I have it mentally divided into seven sections. Not only that, there are actually subsections too. Some might label me a bit obsessive.

At section 1.5, there is a bridge over the creek. That is always where we make our first stop. While Willow explores the area, I normally lean on the bridge and watch the water. A little stream flows gently out from the pond, producing peaceful rhythms and little sparkles of light. That morning while Willow explored and sniffed around near the pond, I continued to play the incident with Albert over and over in my mind.

Suddenly, I looked up and saw Robert, a tall black man in his 80s. Robert was waving to me, but he was also keeping his distance. He wears a dust mask for allergies even when there is no pandemic, so lately he's been decked out in something that more closely resembles a hazmat suit. But he did come close enough to shout, "Good morning!" and then to ask about my family.

At that moment, something important dawned on me. Something I had never noticed before. Other than the golf course, I typically only see Robert in one other environment—the Belks Community Center during election days. Robert is always sure to vote, and so am I. My guess is that we vote for different candidates, but what matters is that we both vote.

That would make Albert very happy.

So what is the big truth that I felt the Lord was imparting to me? While we have a long way to go on issues of race, we have already come a very long way. A black man and white man cross paths most mornings at, of all places, a golf course in Alabama, happily greeting each other and discussing life. No one is suspicious or resentful or fearful of anyone. And the other place we've repeatedly encountered each other is at the voting booth.

Compare that to my experience of having seen a black man for the first time ever, those 65 years ago. Albert had anxiety about simply talking to me. He was afraid even to look at me for very long, lest his intent be misinterpreted. And he walked away that day being denied his God-given right to vote. Just during my short lifetime, that's a profound amount of change. And it gives me hope that we will make it all the way.

All the way to the destination of total equality, unity, and harmony among races. We have a long way to go, but God cares deeply about this issue. That means he stands ready and willing to help us. And if we can come this far, why can't we make it the rest of the way?

I believe we can, and with God's help, we will.

TWO

The Blessing of Finding Out You're Wrong

Several years back, we moved from Annapolis, Maryland, to Tuscaloosa, Alabama. It wasn't a huge culture shock for us because I had lived here before while attending the University of Alabama back in the 1970s. Shortly after we moved here, there was a relatively small event that occurred on the golf course, and it involved my friend, Robert. The event was minor, but it illustrates a major principle—one that has the power to change minds and shape destinies.

In fact, the event was so significant to me at the time, that I wrote out a detailed account of it. Keep in mind that I had a different dog back then, Maggie. She was also a German Shepherd, and by this point, she was starting to show some age. She was a sweetheart who had a way of converting people who were afraid of dogs. Once they met her, they somehow became dog lovers—or at least Maggie lovers. Here is how I recorded the event five years ago:

On most mornings, Maggie and I walk about four miles. Most of it is around the Tall Pines Golf Course. Maggie is my ten-year-old German Shepherd. Back when we first started our morning walks, I met a nice, elderly fellow named Van. Van is a retired science teacher and he's pushing 80. He goes in a clockwise direction and I go counterclockwise, so I run into him most mornings, sometimes twice depending on our speed.

Quite often, Van and I will stop and chat, solving world problems before breakfast. If you sense things are getting better, that means Van and I had a productive meeting.

There is another man who walks the course at that same hour. Robert is a black fellow in his late 70s. Most young folks would be proud to walk at Robert's pace. He's a tall man who wears rubber boots with his pants tucked inside them. He also wears a dust mask, I assume to help with allergies.

Robert would wave each morning, but he would always keep his distance. Many times, he has to change his course in order to maintain his distance, but he never fails to keep a healthy amount of green in between us. He obviously did not want to come socialize, so I never pushed the issue.

Maybe he just wants to enjoy some alone time in the mornings, I thought. I can certainly understand that. But it did cross my mind that the presence of Maggie might have been causing him some level of discomfort.

It's well known that in the racial unrest of the 1960s, German Shepherds were used by police in the south against black people. There are iconic images which show police dogs being used to intimidate and terrorize civil rights demonstrators. I couldn't help but wonder if it was Maggie making Robert feel uneasy.

About eight months ago, Robert and I rounded the same corner going in opposite directions. There we were face to face, and Robert had no easy way to politely avoid us. His demeanor was one of apprehension. To put it bluntly, he was afraid of Maggie, and it showed.

Maggie turned and looked at me as if to say, "Okay, Dad, what is the plan here?"

Wanting to put Robert at ease, and not having a lot of time to think through my reaction, I calmly said, "Maggie, be nice and go say hi."

She lowered her ears, put her head down, and started walking slowly up to Robert, her tail in a slow wag. She sort of tilted her head to the side, displaying total submission as she gingerly approached him. Then she gently rubbed up against his leg kind of like a cat would. At that point, she lifted her chin, inviting Robert to pet or scratch if he was so inclined.

Robert reached down and petted Maggie. He was visibly relieved. He petted her for a minute or two as

.her, and then we went our separate

days later, we met Robert again out on the
Instead of avoiding us, this time he waved and
.ded briskly in our direction. He got within 20
yards or so and Maggie trotted over to greet him. He
smiled, petted her, and talked to her for a minute.
Robert had found a new friend.

We decided to walk together for a while, and
Robert spoke up, "You know, I have been avoiding
you all this time because I was afraid of your dog. I'm
glad I know now that she is friendly and nice."

"Maggie invalidated your assumptions, didn't
she?" I politely asserted. Robert looked at me like I
had three heads. He thought for a moment, and then a
smile came across his face.

"I guess she did," he agreed, laughing.

Robert no longer avoids us. Instead, he comes and
seeks us out, and we always enjoy his company.

Last week, Van and I were pushing through some
major world issues. I don't want to seem too
presumptuous, but it felt like the kind of discussion
that might interest heads of state, or maybe the Nobel
prize committee (committee members, please feel free
to contact me for more details).

We were down by the south end of the pond near
the 16th tee box. Robert walked nearby and shifted his
direction to head toward us. Maggie walked over to
Robert so she could escort him back up to where Van
and I were standing. Robert then proceeded to give

both Van and me a warm handshake followed by a big hug.

The hug was unexpected, but nice. Robert joined in the discussion with us. We learned more about our new friend that day. He is a retired educator who graduated from Stillman College, a historically black college in Tuscaloosa. Robert taught in the Greene County School System for many years and then retired as an administrator. There we were, three old guys enjoying nature and each other's company on a sunny Alabama morning. That is how life is supposed to be—filled with precious moments where we connect with and enjoy other people.

Robert and I have been friends for over five years now. Maggie died in June of 2018, and a short time later, we got Willow (our current German Shepherd that I mentioned previously). Robert got a big kick out of meeting Willow for the first time, when she was still a little bundle of fur.

Several weeks ago, I noticed Robert walking toward me on the street where I live. He had never gone that route before. It had been quite a while since I've seen him, as we must have been on different walking schedules of late. I mentioned that I was surprised to see him on our street. He answered, "It's been such a long time since I've seen you and Willow, I came this way hoping to run into you."

How cool is that? I love my friend Robert, and I think he loves Willow and me.

Our friendship and our nice moments on the golf course never would have happened if Robert's erroneous assumption about German Shepherds had not been invalidated. He wouldn't have walked over, and we wouldn't have gotten to know each other.

Another important point about this whole episode is that Robert never would have chosen to have his assumption invalidated. He wouldn't have chosen to come and meet Maggie and pet her. It just happened—caused by an accidental encounter.

Since that time, I have often used the story of Robert and Maggie to illustrate an important point: We all need to check our assumptions. This is a great principle in general, but it's especially important in regard to issues of race. Erroneous assumptions are the root cause of many problems in regard to race relations. They affect how we view people of different color, and usually not in a good way.

The solution?

We all need to make a conscious, ongoing effort to expose our own faulty assumptions. In so doing, we will often clear our hearts and minds of garbage.

Being an engineer by training, I know that one of the best ways to check whether something is true or false, structurally sound or faulty, is to run a test. One simple and effective way to test your assumptions about people of other races is simply to spend time with them.

Just hang out together, and make sure you take time

to listen to them. Don't listen just to respond. Listen to understand exactly what they are saying. More importantly, listen and try to understand what they might be feeling. This can be tough, but it's certainly worth the effort.

Good things come from challenging assumptions.

THREE

The Washington Redskins

Several years after I met Albert, my mother married a man named Ray Carswell. Ray worked at the government printing office in Washington DC, so we left Oakton and moved to Springfield, Virginia, which was a little closer to Ray's job.

Springfield was a little more pretentious than Oakton. I don't mean that in a bad way, it's just true. It was more affluent and sophisticated. I definitely felt a little country by comparison to the people there. Most of my friends parents were college graduates. If not military officers, they worked in some type of white-collar professional career.

Although my mom's parents were college graduates, she grew up during the Great Depression. Sending kids to college was not an option for her family, so we had working-class roots. Moving to Springfield changed my life in many ways. It was a different arena and a different culture—one with a lot more opportunity.

My stepfather, Ray, was a wonderful man. When my mom started dating again, she had several suitors. Most of them wanted me out of the way and it was typical for me to entertain myself while they went out on a date. That was the norm and I had gotten used to it by the time Ray came along.

Imagine my surprise when the first time I ever met Ray, he brought me a Roy Seivers baseball bat. I was a big fan of all Washington sports teams, and Roy was the star first baseman for the Washington Senators.

After getting the bat, I had settled in on the couch for an evening alone when Ray hit me with his second surprise. "Boy, if you plan to go with us, you best go get dressed."

I was ready in a flash!

After some time, it was down to Ray and one other man. Both of my mom's major suitors proposed marriage around the same time, and she asked me to decide between the two. "Are you kidding me? Ray Carswell!" It was no contest.

As I mentioned, I was a huge fan of Washington sports teams, and football was no exception. The Washington Redskins were a major passion in my twelve-year-old life. Not long after we had moved to Springfield, the Redskins were planning to go from the old Griffith Stadium to the brand new DC Stadium (later renamed RFK Stadium).

However, there was a fly in the ointment. DC Stadium was actually owned by the federal government due to its location. Beyond that, the Redskins were in the most politically prominent city in our nation, yet they'd never had a black player on the team. All of the other NFL teams had long since integrated, with the last one going all the way back to 1955. Six years later, the Redskins were still the only segregated NFL team, and it was completely by choice.

Their owner, George Preston Marshall, was accurately portrayed by the media as a flaming racist. As a response to the criticism, Marshall dug in his heels. He vowed that he would not have a black player on his team, and even famously said he would sign black players when the Harlem Globetrotters signed white players.

A confrontation was brewing.

By 1962 Attorney General Robert Kennedy and Secretary of the Interior Steward Udall decided to force the issue.[1] They told Marshall to add a black player to his team or they would revoke his lease. The old stadium had already been torn down, so this was a case of shrewd negotiation.

Marshall had fought this for years, but he was finally beat. He had no other option, and authorized Redskins head coach Bill McPeak to draft black players in the 1962 NFL draft.[2] McPeak chose Ernie Davis—a famous black running back, Heisman winner, and highly coveted pro prospect—as the number one overall pick.

The drama continued, however, when it came to light that the Redskins had secretly agreed to trade away Davis to the Cleveland Browns. That officially made eighth-round draft choice Ron Hatcher the first black player to sign a contract with the Redskins. Although Hatcher was on the roster and he was black, there was no way he'd be good enough to beat out the existing players. It was a major disappointment for those who hoped to see a superstar like Ernie Davis as the Redskins' first black player.

Fortunately, it turned out that the Redskins had traded Davis in exchange for Bobby Mitchell. Bobby was black and a pretty good player. Mitchell went on to have an amazing breakout year in the receiver position for the Redskins. He caught 72 passes for 1,384 yards, the highest of any NFL receiver for 1962 (a feat he repeated the next season). He was an All-Pro for the Redskins and was later inducted into the NFL Hall of Fame.

But his legacy did not end there. He actually became one of the first black NFL executives, spending his entire career of 41 years with the Redskins. Bobby Mitchell passed away in April of 2020, right around the same time I was feeling the call to write this book. He was a wonderful man and a hero to many, including this old Redskins fan.

Interestingly enough, it was the Redskins' prior year season opener that has burned itself into my memory, but not for any good reason. I witnessed a small glimpse of ugly racial history as it was being made, and that is the reason I am writing about all of these events.

The Redskins were all set for opening day of the 1961 season at the new DC stadium. The New York Giants were going to be in town to face off with the Redskins, and my stepfather had bought three tickets.

One for me, one for him, and one for my new Springfield buddy, Woody Hinkle.

After a short wait that felt like forever, game day finally arrived. Woody and I were beyond excited. Ray drove us downtown, and then the three of us had a short walk to the stadium. As we approached, we noticed that there were some kind of protestors outside the stadium.

George Lincoln Rockwell and his American Nazi Party were there in support of the Redskins owner. He was still holding tightly to his racist stance at that point, even though he was under a lot of criticism. The protestors were dressed up as apes and held signs that said, "We want to play too." At that time, this fledgling political party was headquartered in Arlington, Virginia, so I guess they decided to take the short drive over to the stadium to spread their nonsense.

As it turned out, Y.A. Tittle and his New York Giants mounted an amazing comeback against quarterback Norm Snead and the Redskins, winning the game 24-21. I'm sure we weren't too happy about that.

Beyond the football game that day, I remember the protest. George Lincoln Rockwell ended up being shot dead about 5 years later, but not before he and his goons had made an impression on this young man. One of the very odd things about this demonstration is that I don't recall ever hearing any media coverage of it.

Can you imagine today if self-proclaimed American Nazis dressed up as gorillas in order to defend a racist NFL owner?

About 20 years or so ago, I noticed that a long-time

sportswriter for the Washington Times was retiring. His email was listed in the announcement, so I popped him a note recalling the demonstration. Not being able to find anything about it, I had begun to wonder if it had really happened, or if I had just imagined it.

Wanting a little confirmation that it had happened at least roughly according to my recollection, I sought out the help of someone who had surely been there that day. He confirmed that the event had indeed happened, but did not add any detail. Perhaps there was so much shame about the Redskins' past, and the protest itself, that no one wanted to talk about it. Maybe no one even really wanted to think about it.

But it happened.

Imagine if black kids had been walking by that day. How would they have felt? I don't know what it's like to have someone denigrate me and basically label me an animal because of my race. I hope I never have to experience anything like that. But I want to understand.

We should all want to understand.

FOUR

Scared in America

By the time I met Butch Lacey, it had been roughly a decade since my experience with Albert. During that time, I had not had any meaningful relationships with black people. I saw them on TV. Martin Luther King, Jr., and many others had been working tirelessly for civil rights. But none of that really affected me, to be honest. At least I didn't perceive it to affect me.

The only relevant experience I can recall in high school was trying to reach out to the black students in my school. I had been the student body president, and I remember reaching out to see if they wanted to get involved in various activities. They were scared, and tried as much as possible to keep to themselves. I didn't understand at the time, but that's because I didn't know what it's like to a black teenager. In the 1960s. In Virginia. In a high school of 2,000 people—and 1,998 of them are white.

Short of finding those two black students and asking them how they felt, I can only try to imagine what they went through. Suffice it to say, their high school experience was clearly a lot different from mine. But I just could not relate at the time. The reality of what it must have been like for them was something that apparently just escaped me.

So again, I didn't have any relationships with black people, and I hardly had any experiences with them at all. But I did have some personal experiences that ultimately led up to me meeting Butch and being blessed with my first ever black friend.

In 1961, my Boy Scout troop was selected to march in John F. Kennedy's inauguration parade. It was a cold, snowy, windy day. A buzz had gotten around that the United States Naval Academy would also be marching in the parade, and that Joe Bellino would be there. Joe had been a star running back at Navy, and was the Heisman trophy winner that year.

Several of us broke away and scurried off to see if we could meet Bellino. We actually found him and he was very nice to our little group of scouts, letting us take pictures. My stepdad, Ray, had his own darkroom. So I made several copies of the photo and later sent them to Bellino, along with a request for him to autograph one and send it back.

He gladly obliged. If he had not already been my hero before that, he definitely was now. I wanted to be like Joe Bellino, and that meant I would need to get appointed to the US Naval Academy.

Turning 17 years old in 1965, I was now eligible to enlist in the US Naval Reserve. I promptly did so. My new job working for the federal government would nearly double the income I received from my lawn-mowing ventures each month, but more importantly, it would help my chances of getting in the door at Annapolis.

Entering the Naval Reserve involved standing in a line for processing. The processing line is where I met Butch for the first time, and we were instant pals. Standing in line next to each other, we figured out that we were also the youngest guys there. Most of the enlistees were likely signing up as an alternative to being drafted and ending up in the jungles of Vietnam.

After processing, the first order of business is boot camp at Great Lakes Naval Training facility, located in the Chicago area. Since both Butch and I were still in high school, we had to wait until summer for boot camp. But after processing, we were officially known as "seaman recruits" until we had the chance to complete boot camp.

Butch and I got to attend boot camp together. When we first arrived, we were two teenagers set loose in the big city of Chicago—no adult supervision. I know we did not fly, but I can't recall if our transportation was a bus or a train. All I remember is that we got there a day early, and that meant we would have a chance to enjoy some night life.

After getting a cheap hotel (maybe the YMCA), we decided to go out on the town. Having no extra clothes turned out to be good fortune. We donned our uniforms, complete with the spiffy white sailor hats, and went bar hopping. It didn't seem to matter that we were underage, no one troubled us for IDs in light of the sailor uniforms.

After enjoying ample spirits, we decide to hop the trains and tour the city a little. Maybe not the best idea for a couple of 17-year olds who had never been away from home before. I remember walking past a group of rough looking men and one of them said, "Ah, they're just sailors. They don't have any money. Let's leave them alone."

Apparently that wasn't enough to help us recognize our own naiveté. Instead, it took a Chicago police officer later walking up to us, his face covered with horror. "What in the _____ _____ are you two idiots doing here? This is the worst part of Chicago. You guys will get killed down here! You need to get out of here now!"

With that directive, he personally escorted us back to our hotel. He wasn't leaving the decision up to us. Plus, we'd already had enough fun, especially for two kids who needed to be sharp when reporting to boot camp early the next morning.

Butch and I both survived boot camp and made it safely back home. I don't recall us having any tours of Chicago night life after that one episode. Maybe we gained some wisdom at Great Lakes. After boot camp, we ended up in the same reserve unit, which met one evening per week as I recall.

There was also one weekend per month, and two

weeks active training each year. On one of those training exercises, we were in Norfolk, Virginia, playing around on some ship. Whenever we had time off, you could find our gang at one of the Norfolk bars. I recall one such visit when some of the locals made some nasty comments to Butch. They failed to account for the fact that Butch had a literal boat load of sailors in there with him.

We'll just say that Butch came out on top in that little incident.

My friend and I parted ways in late spring of 1966. The commanding officer of our reserve unit learned of the order for me to enter the Naval Academy, and he informed the rest of the group. That meant I would no longer be with the unit. That meeting was the last time I ever saw Butch.

He was my first ever black friend, and I often wonder what became of him. I wish I had the chance to talk with him again. If I had the chance, I would ask him more about how he felt on a particular spring day in 1965.

Butch and I were with a busload of sailors passing over the Potomac. We were on our way to the Marine Corps base in Quantico, Virginia, to learn how to shoot rifles. Several minutes had gone by since we had heard anything from Butch. Butch was the only black member of this motley crew that comprised our naval reserve unit from Washington, DC.

Butch was normally high energy—always talking with others and cutting up. But at this moment, his silence was deafening.

"Hey, what's the deal with you?" I asked my friend, playfully.

"I have never been this far south before. I'm scared," Butch explained.

Thinking he was joking, I laughed out loud. Then I realized he wasn't joking. He was visibly shaking with fear. I still didn't understand, but I at least knew that there wasn't anything funny happening.

Thankfully, Butch made it through our trip just fine. He was around friends, and none of us were mingling with the native Virginians. Shooting guns and hanging around with pals was just too much fun. Well, maybe for everyone except Butch. But the point is, we all stayed to ourselves, so there were no comments or incidents of any kind. Still, I have to admit that I don't know what the experience was like for him.

How can I? I haven't walked a mile in his shoes. I've never been sitting on a bus, the only person of my race present, scared to go any further because of the color of my skin. Sadly, it never occurred to me back then to just stop and ask him more about how he felt. If anything, I probably just tried to help take his mind off of it.

I wonder if that's something we often do in these situations. Do we try to smooth over anything that makes us uncomfortable, diverting attention elsewhere? What about the person who doesn't have that luxury? Maybe myself and the rest of the guys tried to divert the focus to other topics. We were probably trying to make Butch feel better. After telling him not to worry, maybe we just sort of moved on toward the weekend's activities. But I wonder now if Butch really moved on. I wonder how he really felt on the rest of that trip.

I have to admit, I really don't know what it's like to be scared for my life while driving across America.

Butch knows.

FIVE

The United States Naval Academy

A Special Man

"What the heck are you doing, Covington? Get your _____ eyes in the boat! Are you looking around to try to buy this place?"

It was the summer of 1966, affectionately known as "plebe summer." This must have been on a weekend, because we weren't sitting with our normal squads. After noon meal formation on Saturdays, the thing to do was head over to the mess hall and wander around looking for a place to sit.

If you were a plebe (which is the Naval Academy equivalent of 'freshman'), this was a very important decision. Mealtimes were stressful anyway, and you did whatever you could to minimize your pain. You simply couldn't afford to sit down at a table where there was a jerk at the head seat who thought it was his job to terrorize you.

On this particular day, I had obviously failed.

The proper table manners were for plebes to sit down using only the two inches of the chair closest to the edge. Back straight. Chin tucked. Eye lock forward.

That's actually what was meant by the term "eyes in the boat." You weren't to be looking around. By the way, the proper response to this jerk's question, would have been "Sir! No Sir!"

An improper response would have been, "Do you have change for a quarter?" Don't ask me how I know.

On another weekend, I was chopping around (trotting with your chin tucked in) the mess hall trying to scope out my least painful lunch experience. All of a sudden this guy yells, "Hey, you! Sit over here by me!" In a now familiar pattern in my life, I look up to see the only black person I had ever personally run into at Annapolis —Midshipman 2C, Charles Bolden.

He was also the first black person who had ever been in any form of authority over me. Stopping at the seat next to his, I stood, along with everyone else, until after the prayer. At that point, we were given official permission to sit down.

"Brigade, seats!"

Mr. Bolden was sitting at the head of the table. Even though I was not allowed to look directly at him, I could see through my peripheral vision that he was smiling. "So, Mr. Covington, tell me about yourself."

But the kindness didn't stop there. He also gave all of us plebes at the table "carry-on" which meant we did not have to do the awkward and tiring brace up thing while eating. This was a really good table.

The other thing I quickly noticed about Mr. Bolden was that he had an air of confidence which separated him from the others. He wasn't insecure, and trying to prove himself. He wasn't trying to lord his authority over anyone. For that matter, I didn't see him intimidate, harass, coerce, or browbeat anyone, ever. My sense was that he was different—special even.

My young intuition about Charles proved to be correct. Charles Bolden retired as a Marine Corps Major General. He had a very long and distinguished military career. He was also an astronaut who flew on four space shuttle missions. And if all that wasn't enough, he was appointed as Administrator of NASA during President Obama's first term, becoming the first black person to ever hold the position.

There's so much to admire about people like him who stared down hate, prejudice, and injustice and said, "I think I'm going to rise above you."

Congratulations, Mr. Bolden.

You did it.

Terrorized and Broken

By the fall of 1967, I was in my second year, classified as a 3C sophomore. The designation of class, such as plebe, sophomore, etc., was more than just a way to identify what year you were in. Each year's class had a different role at the Academy. As a 4C, you were a bottomfeeder— the lowest of the low.

By the time you got to 3C, you just tried to keep yourself as much as possible. There was no good reason to draw attention to yourself. The primary interaction you might initiate with others was to be helpful to the plebes, sort of like a mentor. It wasn't that you would befriend the plebes. That was not a good idea, but you could give them some sage advice on occasion.

The Naval Academy divides people in to companies. Each company has roughly 30 members of each year's class, adding up to about 120 midshipmen total. In my company, I noticed again a familiar pattern. The incoming plebe class that year had one black guy. We'll call him "Don."

A hot shot running back, Don had been recruited for the Navy football team. If I'm not mistaken, he was originally from a northern state. There was only one problem for Don.

He had attitude.

Many white folks at the time probably would have referred to him as "uppity." Having an attitude in the Naval Academy, especially as a plebe, is just not a good idea for anyone. At least not if you wanted any kind of peace.

Companies are further divided into squads, and Don was in my squad. Previously, I had mentioned wandering around looking for a place to sit at mealtime. That only happened on the weekends. Sunday night through Friday evening, you always ate with your squad. The seating arrangement was such that each table had four plebes, four 3C classmen, two 2C classmen, and two 1C classmen. So in the more familiar vernacular, there were four freshman, four sophomores, two juniors, and two seniors at each table.

During mealtimes, plebes were usually grilled on whether or not they knew required information. For a plebe, any mealtime that could be escaped without a "come around" was a raging success. A come around was a form of punishment. Basically if you didn't know required information, or you did something out of line, or you said something stupid, you got a come around.

The come around basically meant you would have to go to the room of the upper classmen who had caught you being unprepared or doing something dumb. When you got there, they would run you ragged, give you all kinds of tough or denigrating tasks to complete, verbally assault you, and basically just give you an all-around hard time.

But Don was definitely getting an atypical number of come arounds, much more than the normal share. I felt bad for Don. He seemed to bring a lot of the trouble on himself because of his attitude. He must have realized the way I felt about him, because he seemed drawn to my roommate and me.

We would often talk to him, give him advice, and we were just generally nice to him. No matter Don's attitude, he definitely didn't deserve what happened to him a couple of months into his first year at the Academy.

One night, Don came running into our room. He was hysterical, and it was the middle of the night. As we woke up and shook off the heaviness of sleep, it became apparent that he had been terrorized by some of the upperclass midshipmen.

They had come into his room donning sheets fashioned to look like Ku Klux Klan outfits. I was horrified then, and I am just as horrified now. As I write this, I'm realizing it's the first time I've ever recorded the event. It was terrible.

Don was essentially a broken man after that. They broke him. If that's what they wanted, they got it. Because his personality changed. He withdrew into a shell for a time, and then resigned from the Academy before the semester ended. A man's future, his life, his career, his education, was all put into severe jeopardy because some goons thought it was a good idea to terrorize him for his race.

The men who terrorized him probably went on to graduate and serve as Naval or Marine Corps officers. They were probably recognized as men of honor.

In another familiar pattern of my life, I have to stop and admit something. When I went into the Naval Academy, there were plenty of other people of my race. I didn't feel singled out in any way because of my race. That means I don't know what it is like to be the only black guy of 30 people in my company's plebe class. I don't understand the threat to safety and well-being that Don must have felt. I don't understand the insecurity it might have caused him.

I don't know what it's like to have my future and my career derailed because of my race. And I don't know what it's like to have someone come into my room in the middle of the night, wearing an outfit that essentially says, "We're here to murder you because of your race." I hope I never have to experience anything like that. But I want to understand.

We should all want to understand.

The Preaching Sailor

My mother and stepfather were good people. My mother had a deep faith in God, and that faith drove her to value and honor all people regardless of their background, race, economic status, etc. It was very important to her, and I realize now that it must have rubbed off on me.

Fortunately, they were on the right side of the Civil Rights movement. Justice and treating people fairly were big issues with them and with me. That led to me being pretty outspoken politically. The country was absolutely failing at that time on matters of race. There was injustice everywhere, and obviously, I often witnessed it in my personal life.

As wonderful as Ray and mom were, they did something a little funky during my plebe year. They moved without telling me where they were moving! I'm sure they didn't mean to, and they will probably deny it till the end of time. But all they told me is that they might move to Florida. Imagine my surprise when I found out they had moved to Mobile, Alabama, of all places! Nothing destroys a kid's self-confidence like his parents running away from home.

All kidding aside, an interesting thing happened when I got to visit them in Mobile during the Christmas holiday of 1967. We were United Methodists, and the Methodists had a tradition during the Christmas season that one Sunday service would be run by college students.

The pastor thought it would be a good idea for me to give the sermon that Sunday. I have no idea why. But I agreed, and decided to talk about race relations. Let's just say my talk was not going to be pleasant for anyone—especially not anyone in this all-white church. In Alabama. In 1967.

Ray reviewed my sermon notes and went into a rage. "You can't say that stuff here! Your mother and I actually have to live here!"

His reaction took me by surprise. Neither Ray nor my mom had ever tried to censor anything I said about issues of race. But he was obviously feeling the heat on this one. Who can blame him? Most of the time in life, it's not our initial reaction to tough situations that define us. Once we've had time to calm down—to think and pray through everything—that shows who we really are.

Several minutes passed, and Ray came back in the room. He sat down across from me, looked me in the eye, and said, "I'm sorry. You're right. Everything you're saying is right. You deliver that message. I'm proud of you."

Sunday morning came, and as I delivered my sermon, you could hear a pin drop. I do not have any of my notes from the sermon I preached that day. But as best I can recall, these were the topics I covered:

(1) I noted that as I looked around, I saw no black faces in the room. I questioned why that was the case. Was it a heart issue?

(2) Discrimination based on race is wrong. It is not in line with God's teaching, which is to love everyone and treat everyone well.

(3) God embraces justice. It's of paramount importance to him. We should also embrace justice.

(4) The events in Birmingham with police dogs and fire hoses were wrong, and should be condemned by all people of good conscience.

Fortunately for me, the respect for our military runs so deep that it's really hard for most people to get mad at someone in a white Navy uniform—even if they are delivering a message that's very hard to hear.

Beyond the dead silence, the only real response I can recall was that everyone was generally nice and polite afterward. This one little old lady did come up to me afterward to say, "Young man, you must be from up north."

"No ma'am. I am from Virginia—about as southern as you can get."

The New Naval Academy

In the mid-1980s, I was out of the Navy and working in manufacturing. My family and I moved to Maryland so that I could take a job as plant manager for a Sherwin-Williams facility. We lived close to the Naval Academy for nearly thirty years, sponsoring and mentoring midshipmen for about ten of those years. I'm happy to say that even as far back as the 80s, the Naval Academy had already made tremendous progress.

Many of the midshipmen we had in our home were black. All of the ones we had in our home were like children to me and my wife, Linda. And our daughter, Leigh, thought of them as brothers.

For those ten years, we lived in chaotic bliss with Leigh's teenage friends and a herd of midshipmen at our house every weekend. The fun would begin on Friday evening and run through Sunday evening meal formation, when the young men had to be back at the Academy.

Doug and Drew were a couple of midshipmen that often hung around our home. Doug was from New York and Drew was from Florida. Drew had gotten himself a 1960s vintage Volkswagen bus, the iconic one often owned by hippies. The front passenger floorboard was totally rusted out, and this van actually had three engines —none of which were installed.

Of course, all of this was a big mess, but we let him store it at our house anyway. Unfortunately, we had neighborhood covenants and it was getting to be a bit of a problem. It was driving the neighbors nuts, to be frank. Linda and I weren't too thrilled about it either after a while.

One cold February Saturday morning, I left out for work. Doug and Drew were staying with us for the weekend. I came home around lunch time and Doug met me in the driveway.

Now, Doug is always happy. If you look up the word "joyful" in the dictionary, there's a picture of Doug's face. He's just that kind of guy. But that day, his demeanor was serious.

"Mr. Covington, there's something wrong with your electrical system. The breaker keeps tripping."

Being a cranky old engineer, I have well defined methods for problem solving. The first thing I do is ask, "What has changed?" So my next thought was, "The electrical system was working just fine when I left this morning. What has changed is that you two clowns are now awake."

It didn't take long to diagnose the problem. The temperature was about minus 7 outside that day. The bus was backed into our garage and the garage doors were wide open. They had two space heaters going full blast in an attempt to heat all of Anne Arundel County.

"So, how did you guys do in circuits?" I inquired, referring to an electrical engineering class, before pointing them toward the source of the problem.

While that may not be the most riveting story you've ever heard, I do have a point. Those are the only kinds of memories I have from that time period. We spent a decade from the early 80s to the early 90s hosting all kinds of midshipmen in our home—midshipmen of all races—and we never once heard of or dealt with any problem that involved mistreatment of black people. I'm not saying racial problems didn't exist at all for the Naval Academy during those years. But clearly, they were not as prevalent as when I had been there.

Four Brothers

There were four members of the class of 1990 that we will never forget. Todd was the son of another Sherwin-Williams plant manager, who was my friend and colleague. Todd's roommate was Joe. Todd and Joe had two buddies that often accompanied them, Andy and Everett. Todd and Joe were both white, Andy and Everett were both black.

One of the things I often told the midshipmen was that when I was out of town on business, they were responsible for harassing Leigh's dates. Fortunately for me, these young men take assignments seriously.

During one of my business trips, Leigh was set to attend a Capitals hockey game with a young man she had met at school. Of course, when he came to the door, my daughter was not yet ready to go. The midshipmen met him at the door, ushered him into the living room, and promptly began to interrogate him.

"Where are you going?"

"Um, to a hockey game—sir."

"What hockey game?"

"The Capitals."

"Good, we have tickets to that game. Where are you sitting?"

"Can I grab you a beer? What kind do you like?"

"Um, I'm too young to drink, sir."

"Good answer."

And that continued on for quite a while until Leigh rescued the poor fellow by showing up in the living room. On their way out to the car, the young man was still visibly shaken.

"Are those your brothers?"

"Seriously? Did you even look at them? One white guy with flaming red hair. One white guy who is extremely tall. And two black guys. You think we're all related? But yeah, they're kind of like brothers. Let's go have fun now."

Overcorrection Creates New Challenges

During Drew's senior year, one issue of race did come to light. The Brigade of Midshipmen (which is what they call the collective student body) at the Naval Academy is organized much like the rest of the military. The Brigade is divided into six battalions. There are five companies in each battalion. Each company has a company commander, and they all report up to the Brigade Commander, a 1C midshipmen who is chosen for outstanding leadership performance.

The higher up you are in the command structure, the more gold stripes you have on your sleeve or shoulder board. The stripes matter. They are not just symbolic. In many ways, they reflect your class ranking, and your class ranking determines who gets picked first in service selection.

Service selection refers to the job you get in the military. There are only so many assignments available in aviation, submarines, the Marine Corps, or whatever other area you might have in mind for your future. The Navy's need, along with your class ranking, will determine where you end up—perhaps defining your entire career. Class ranking is important, to state it mildly, and the Naval Academy had just announced their list of "stripers" for that year.

Drew had lots of data to show that the selection had been biased. Blacks and women completely dominated the selection even though they made up a small percentage of possible candidates, and Drew was upset. The superintendent of the Academy at that time had actually been at the Naval Academy with me. Though I did not personally know him, he had been a football star and everyone at the Academy knew who he was.

But I was not a big fan of the job he was doing as superintendent of the academy at this time. He had made some public comments concerning the Naval Academy that I thought were off base. It seemed obvious that there was social engineering going on at the Academy. To put it bluntly, it seemed obvious that people were being chosen primarily because they were black or female.

Yes, they had certainly worked hard. But so had a lot of other people. And when the selection is all tilted in the favor of certain groups—especially after comments indicating it would be that way—it's pretty easy to see what's happening. It would have been easy to pile on this superintendent in my answer to Drew. But the superintendent may not have been the one who made the decision.

"Drew, there is probably a lot we do not know. Maybe the admiral made this decision, or maybe it came from the very top of the Navy—or even higher."

Of course, this did not make Drew feel any better. He and others were in competition with their classmates. They had worked very hard for certain perks and class position, and they were now being put at a disadvantage because they were white males. There are only so many slots. Is it right to award those slots based on anything other than merit?

I don't know what it's like to work very hard and then get passed over for a promotion just because I am a white male. As far as I know, that's never happened to me. I don't understand what that's like and I hope I never have to experience it. The main point here? I'm not sure that this is the best route to go. Creating new racial problems through overcorrection of previous ones seems like a recipe for disaster to me.

———

A year or so after we stopped sponsoring midshipmen, the head of leadership development at the academy wanted to buy me lunch. I had written several books on leadership, and he had read one of them.

We met at one of my favorite places in Severna Park, a little Italian restaurant called Mezzonotti's. I have forgotten the man's name, so we'll call him Phil. Phil, a Marine Corps Major, was very polite and friendly. We were deep into a great conversation when all of a sudden he got a phone call. He was quite concerned.

"John, I am so sorry, but I have to run back to the academy. We have an honor offense I need to deal with. It's a black female, and this is her 6th honor offense."

"Are you kidding me?" I thought to myself. "Six?" It used to be that someone was discharged from the academy after one honor offense. One. But somehow this midshipman has six? The major did not have to give any further explanation. It was obvious that there was a reason he had offered up information about the midshipman's race and gender.

I squinted my eyes a tad, "She's going to graduate, isn't she?"

"You bet! Short of murdering someone, she will be commissioned as an officer in the Navy."

Honor had always been a cornerstone at the Naval Academy, and all the service academies. At West Point, a cadet could be discharged simply for knowing about an honor offense committed by someone else, and then failing to report it. At Navy, the rule was less strict. If a midshipman knew about another midshipman's offense, they had the option of counseling them or turning them in. The relevant question they wanted you to ponder before deciding was, "Would I want to serve under this individual?"

Now why does the military stress honor? It's best to illustrate with an example. Let's say you are responsible for taking inventory of weapons prior to your unit going into combat. It's your job, but you forgot to do it. Your commanding officer comes and asks you, "Have you done inventory?"

You fear looking bad or getting into trouble, and you're sure everything is fine. Surely the last person to do inventory did it correctly. So you respond, "Yes, inventory's all done, Sir."

However, what you don't know is that inventory is actually dangerously low. When you get into combat, your unit runs out of weapons. People die—needlessly— as a result of your lie.

That is why honor is so important in the military.

Initially, I was very angry at this situation. But later, I reflected on the fact that no human institution is perfect. Was this female any less deserving of an officer commission than the men who had donned white sheets? Certainly not. The truth is, none of them were deserving, because they had an honor problem. That couldn't have been good for anyone—neither our military as a whole, nor the people who were unjustly commissioned as officers, nor the people who served under them.

The Bible teaches that if you don't discipline a child, it's the equivalent of hating them because it will ultimately lead up to their death.[1] There's a similar principle here. Letting people get away with bad behavior, moral failures, and the like—just because there is some issue involving their race—is the equivalent of hating them. It very well could lead to their death, and the death of others around them. It certainly doesn't do anything good for them or the path they are on in life.

I don't know what it's like to get placed in a position that I did not deserve and was not prepared for. I don't know what it's like to get away with major improprieties and offenses in the United States military just because of the color of my skin. Unlike the other situations I cannot understand, I don't actually want to understand this one. I just wish it weren't so.

Again, I think this kind of thing is a recipe for disaster.

I think we can correct injustice without creating new problems.

Reflection

Which one of those situations bothers you more and why? The black female candidate who was allowed to commit major offenses without being disciplined, or the young men getting away with terrorizing a fellow midshipman because of his race? Ask yourself: Is my response to this story influenced by my race?

SIX

The Greatest Generation

Eons ago, male engineering students were advised to take some social science classes, as that is where all the pretty girls were. However, I never took that many. In fact, I only took one that I can recall, and that was Sociology 101. Interestingly enough, I think I learned a few things.

One of the things I remember learning was the term 'ethnocentric.' If I recall, the main point of the teaching about ethnocentricity is this: Don't judge another person's culture according to the values of your own culture. For fairness, a person should be judged according to the values they've learned in their culture.

So how does that work across different eras? Do we judge people from the past based on the understanding we have today?

To kick off this discussion, I'd like to share a quote from Bruce Hedrick. Bruce is a good friend of mine. He's also a West Point graduate, a Vietnam Combat veteran, and a graduate in chemical engineering from the University of Alabama.

> "Having been born and raised in Birmingham [Alabama], I got to see systemic racism up close and personal. After watching peaceful, non-violent black protestors being attacked by police dogs and fire hoses, I was ashamed to tell folks I was from Birmingham for decades."

As shameful as parts of it may be, we can't change the past. All we can do is study it, reflect on it, try to learn from it, and try to move forward. In that spirit, let's cover some people and events that I'd really rather not think about. But if we can learn, grow, and move forward, it will be worth the trouble.

Eradicating Bigotry from the Family Line

"You know why they have those signs with no words on them don't you? It's because those [n-words] can't read."

My cousin was probably 11 or 12 years old at the time she made that statement to me. Absolutely stunned, I struggled to catch my breath a bit. The adrenaline of confrontation can do that to you. Taking a deep breath, I responded as calmly as I could, explaining to my young cousin how her comment had been wrong. I was around 16 at the time.

Ray had a sister who lived in Birmingham. Even though we were related only by marriage, I considered her and her husband to be my aunt and uncle. Their two daughters were my cousins. It was obvious they had learned this kind of poison from their parents.

Uncle Joe (not his real name) was probably in his mid-forties or early fifties at that time. He was a big man, about 6' 2" and he was totally bald. His face was always red, I'm not sure why. Maybe it was from working out on the railroad. He was an engineer (the guy who drove the train), an avid fisherman, and a BBQ enthusiast who took his secret sauce to the grave.

It was always fun going down to Birmingham for a visit. Our first trip to see these relatives was actually the first time I ever set foot in Alabama, a state I have grown to love.

Uncle Joe and Ray were at the polar opposite ends of the political spectrum. Mom and Aunt Nora (not her real name) tended to stay out of the fray. Not Ray, though. He loved to argue.

Ray would've argued with a stick. Seriously, if you took one side of an issue, he would take the other side just to have the argument. One time we visited when Lyndon Johnson was running against Barry Goldwater. Most people considered it a foregone conclusion that Johnson would soon win in a landslide.

Not ten minutes after our arrival, Uncle Joe and Ray had gotten into an almost violent political argument. After a while Uncle Joe finally yelled, "I will bet you $2000 that Goldwater wins!" Ray remained very calm.

"Mildred, go get the checkbook."

Ray had called his bluff. No bet was made that day.

Another time, their family was visiting us in Springfield. Uncle Joe snuck outside and put a bumper sticker on Ray's car.

WALLACE FOR PRESIDENT

Ray happened to be driving his carpool to DC that day, and all the way in, he noticed that a black truck driver was tailgating him. It was to the point that everyone in the carpool was worried, but fortunately nothing ever came of it.

Ray discovered the bumper sticker when he got to work that day. When he got home, even after a whole day at work, he was more mad than I've ever seen him in my life.

Uncle Joe had joined the Navy in World War II, as had Ray. Uncle Joe actually could not swim. Why in the world would anyone join the Navy if he could not swim? In any event, he was tall enough to fake it during boot camp by staying near the side of the pool. On the sides, near the wall of the pool, he could touch bottom as he drove himself along the length of the pool.

Later, when he was in Hawaii, he and some fellow sailors were ordered into a whale boat. A whale boat looks like a crude bass boat designed to haul quite a few people. So they head out, motoring through the surf, and the guy in charge all of a sudden says, "Everybody out! If you want to get back home—swim!"

Needless to say, Uncle Joe was in a deep mess. Everyone else immediately jumps in and starts swimming for shore. But Uncle Joe's still sitting there. Given a direct order to dive in, he continues to refuse. The man in charge pulls out his side arm, "My orders are to shoot anyone who does not dive in!"

Finally, he had no other option. He just jumped in and immediately began to drown. The boat's driver took pity on him and threw him a donut lifesaver. But he still had to make it back to shore on his own. He lagged everyone else by about an hour, but he somehow passed the test. Sometimes you just need help.

If I had to bet on it, I would wager that Joe was a member of the Klan. The Klan was huge back then, enjoying a resurgence in membership in response to the Civil Rights movement. So it would be my best guess that he was a member. He certainly had bigoted viewpoints, and I did not agree with them.

But he was still my family and I still loved him.

Uncle Joe and his wife passed on many years ago. Several years back, Linda and I were invited to the wedding of their granddaughter. Interestingly enough, she had hit it off with her fiancé after he was visiting their home and noticed one of my books on the table. He said, "Hey, do you all know John Covington?"

A connection was made and the rest is history.

The good news—and the ultimate point of my sharing about Uncle Joe and our family history—is that when we got to the wedding, I noticed many black people in attendance. Not only that, some of them were in prominent positions in the ceremony.

It seems that bigotry did not survive the family line of Uncle Joe.

That begs the question: Was Uncle Joe simply a

product of the culture and environment he grew up in? I don't know the right answer. All I know for sure is that his bigotry was wrong. But that doesn't mean there was nothing at all good about the man.

Reflection

Did you have family members from previous generations who were racist? How do you feel about them as a person? How do you feel about their racist views? Is it possible to separate the two? Regardless of your feelings toward them, do you feel strongly about breaking the cycle of bigotry?

Erasing the Lines Drawn by Past Generations

One of my fondest childhood memories was going to holiday celebrations in Roanoke, Virginia, at Uncle George and Aunt Ruth's house. Aunt Ruth was the oldest of four siblings on my mom's side of the family. She was born either in the late 1880s or early 1890s. Their house in Roanoke was huge. Family outings meant no less than 20 guests, all of which stayed in the one house.

All the bedrooms were upstairs and there was a coal burning furnace in the basement. Hanging around with Uncle George was fun for me. I thoroughly enjoyed doing just about anything with him. Going down to the basement with him to shovel coal was one of my favorites. He always had the sleeves rolled up on his long white dress shirts, especially when there was coal to be shoveled.

Uncle George was a design engineer for the Norfolk and Western Railway. He actually did drafting work on the old steam locomotives. He also was wise enough to buy stock in the original American Telephone and Telegraph (AT&T) early in its history. And he bought a lot of it.

They had more money than the average person would know what to do with, and their solution was to do pretty much nothing with it. They hardly ever spent a dime they didn't have to. I won't say they were prudish, but some of the family wondered how they'd ever had kids, since the two of them wanting to do something as risqué and fun as sex was inconceivable.

As it turns out, the conservative behavior must've been all Uncle George. After he died, Aunt Ruth had an absolute ball. She wasn't going to let any of the money go to waste. She promptly bought a smaller but much nicer house in the fancy part of town, got herself a brand new Mercedes, and went on about every European cruise that existed back then.

Aunt Ruth was exclusively WASP-V, meaning you needed to be a "White Anglo Saxon Protestant Virginian" if you wanted to be on her good side. If you were not a native Virginian, that meant you must have a defect of some kind. When one of her sons married an Episcopalian, she nearly disowned him—that was just too close to Catholic for her. Their pastors even wear the priest uniforms!

Her poor daughter-in-law, Lucy, was never quite good enough for her. It eventually got to the point that no one wanted to be around Aunt Ruth. Maybe it was because we were WASP-V, and therefore never caught Aunt Ruth's bad side, but somehow Linda and I still got along with her fine. We normally invited her to spend holidays with us. Otherwise she would have spent them alone.

We're still waiting on the family royalties from the movie *Driving Miss Daisy* because we're sure it was based on Aunt Ruth. She actually had a black male helper named Randolph, the equivalent of "Hoak" played by Morgan Freeman. Each morning, Aunt Ruth would fix herself a bowl of oatmeal and most mornings she also fixed one for Randolph. He did not live with her, but he came over most days and just sort of did whatever she needed, little odds and ends around the house mostly.

He could not have been much younger than Aunt Ruth, and eventually age caught up with him. He became too feeble to do much good as a handy man. Still, he came around anyway and had breakfast with Aunt Ruth most mornings. They would sit at her breakfast table and talk for hours.

Isn't it strange that a person can hold negative views about an entire race of people—yet in the right context, they can sit and enjoy the company of a member of that race? That was not uncommon in previous generations. They could somehow see the value in a person, yet devalue them in other ways all at the same time, sometimes in the same breath.

One thing I often wonder about Aunt Ruth. Was race just another point of division for her? Obviously, she categorized people in her mind and heart according to many things. It wasn't enough to be an American. You needed to be a Virginian. It wasn't enough to be Christian. You had to be firmly protestant, and apparently in one of the handful of denominations she actually approved of. There seems to have been a lot more lines and divisions and distinctions for people in general back then, and Aunt Ruth was a strong example of that principle.

Did racist views of bygone generations stem from the fact that they believed in drawing lines just about anywhere and for any reason? Did they just believe in dividing people as a way of determining who was good or bad, worthy or unworthy?

It kind of seems that way.

Say it Ain't So

You've already gotten to know my stepfather a little, but he was a member of "The Greatest Generation" and there are a few other things worth sharing about him.

Ray Crumpton (he hated his middle name) Carswell was born around the turn of the century in Dothan, Alabama. He made his high school football team by tackling the legendary Johnny Mack Brown. Brown went on to play football at the University of Alabama, and was part of their first ever national championship team in 1925. After college, Brown ended up being a film actor who starred in quite a few westerns.

Ray also had an offer to play football at Alabama, but he chose to go to work instead. He was anxious to get into the newspaper business, and went to work straight away for the Dothan Eagle. He did some reporting, but being a small-town newspaper, the Eagle also had him doing some printing work. He might have even delivered a few papers. But he really loved sports, and he spent as much time and effort as possible being a sports reporter.

When WWII broke out, Ray was well in his 30s and therefore did not have to concern himself with the draft. Still, he wanted to do his part so he enlisted in the Navy. He was in the Seabees, which is the term for Naval Construction Battalions, and ended up stationed in the Philippines. The young men serving with him called him "Pops."

He despised the term and challenged the entire group of young men to a foot race. If he were to beat every one of them, they had to stop calling him Pops. That was the deal.

They never called him Pops again.

Ray went through wives like socks. He was married four times in his life—twice to the same woman. I'm pretty sure my mom was his one true love. All I know for sure is, I've never seen a couple more in love than the two of them. He was a wonderful stepdad, and I could not have asked for any better. I don't believe there is a man alive who could have loved me more than Ray did.

One day he was browsing through a Life Magazine—

either that or the Saturday Evening Post. It was one of those big, oversized magazines. In the magazine that month was a large photo of a lynching that occurred in northern Florida. It happened years prior, I believe in the 1930s. After researching, I believe it may have been the lynching of Claude Neal, but I can't be sure.

All I remember for sure is that there was a very graphic picture of a black man hanging from a tree, with some onlookers standing nearby.

Ray stared blankly at the photo.

"I was there," he said stoically. "I was at that lynching."

One of the photographers at the newspaper had gotten word that there was to be a lynching that night in Florida. Dothan is in south Alabama, not too far above the Florida line. He asked Ray if he wanted to go, and obviously Ray had agreed.

After the black man was hung, one of the mob members noticed Ray and his friend. "Who are those guys?" he asked, inciting the mob to turn their attention toward Ray and the photographer.

It quickly came out that they were from the newspaper.

"Get two more ropes and we'll hang them too!"

They grabbed Ray and his friend, but when no more ropes could be found, the mob eventually decided to let them go. He didn't tell me this part, but I imagine it also took some persuasion on Ray and the photographer's part to convince the mob that they weren't a threat.

The day President Kennedy was shot, I saw Ray cry

for the first time I can recall. I do not recall whether he cried telling me this story. Maybe he thought the black man was guilty of some horrible crime, and this was simply a form of justice. Maybe the reporter in Ray was just curious. Maybe he thought it wouldn't really happen. Maybe he was even trying to do something good, like stop the incident or report on it, but was overcome by fear once there. Ray had been pretty young when it happened, maybe he just didn't think very much at all before going.

I don't know why Ray went. He didn't tell me that. But I often wonder, how did he feel about this incident? Did he regret going? Did he regret not trying to stop the lynching? I cannot even imagine.

There's nothing I've written about, ever, that is more gut wrenching than this story. How can men be so evil?

I used to always chide Ray about writing a book. He was a wonderful writer. He never spoke of this incident again, and as a self-absorbed teenager, I guess I was too stupid to ask. While he would sometimes oblige my mom, Ray was not much of a churchgoer and I never heard him talk about his faith. But I think he came to know Jesus and repented of his sins before he passed on.

As much as some people may want me to condemn Ray and say that he was a horrible person due to being at this event, I don't believe that. He wasn't a horrible person. That's the strange thing about human beings. We can be really good one minute, and yet do something really terrible in the next. I'm not equating Ray with the people who organized and carried out the lynching. But his mere presence would make many want to condemn him as evil. I cannot agree with such a sentiment. The Ray I knew was a good father and a good man.

I desperately hope I see Ray again one day. And I hope he and the victim were able to see each other and be reconciled in Heaven.

The last thing I want to add here is this. My stepfather was at the lynching of a black man. That means I was one degree removed from the horror of American lynching. If you and I know each other, that means you are only two degrees removed. Ugly history is still a lot closer than most of us realize.

Hopefully we will all keep moving further and further away.

Honor the Good, Correct the Evil

The Greatest Generation obviously had major issues. However, there's no denying that they accomplished so much that was good and important. What would have happened if they hadn't stepped up to defeat Hitler? Would we all be living in a nightmare—one where a demonically-inspired, German white-supremacist empire rules the entire world? That actually almost happened. But thank God, the greatest generation rose up and overcame.

America has a lot to be thankful for and a lot to be proud of. As Dinesh D'souza often points out, the ugly things in America's past are in every other country's past too. But it's the good things about America that set her apart. The good things simply aren't there for most other nations on earth. In so many ways, it's a wonderful country, and a major blessing to the world.

Still, I do see that there's another side to the American story.

In the introduction, I mentioned the question I had posed to some of my black friends and acquaintances, and that I would share more of their answers later in the book. This one is from my friend Gaston Large. He's an engineering graduate from Alabama.

He has a different perspective on the American flag and many other things American. I'm not saying his perspective is right, or that it is wrong. But I am saying that this is how he feels:

"I remember in the 5th grade, interviewing my Uncle Charles, who served in WWII. I was so excited to hear him talk about it. But when I had to go back and present to my classmates, I was embarrassed. He risked his life fighting for a country that didn't even respect him as a human being. Amongst other things, he talked about how the white soldiers refused to eat with him. But he still felt that his commitment would help bring about change.

During the Vietnam War, my father was drafted into the Army, but after taking a test ended up serving two years in the Navy instead. My dad never talked about it much. I mean, I heard the good stories from him. But about five years ago, I found out that my dad had lived in Mexico. What? How? When?

After coming back home, he could not get a job because of the uniform. Being black didn't help either. He became furious and just wandered around for a while."

I don't know what it's like to fight alongside people on the battlefield, and then have them refuse to eat with me at dinner time. Can you imagine how that made them feel? Can you imagine how their children and grandchildren—the ones who have grown up hearing those stories—still feel about those events?

The flag is meaningful and significant to most of us primarily because of the benefits we associate with it. Freedom. Prosperity. Protection of rights. Safety. Security. Dignity.

The flag may not mean as much to some people because it obviously did not afford them the same benefits.

Reflection

How do you view previous generations and eras? Is there any way to make peace with the ugly parts of our past, and to put it behind us once and for all? What would it take to make that happen? How can we honor the good while also working to correct the evil and injustice?

SEVEN

Making Black Friends Is Not Hard But it Takes Effort

Florence was a black nanny from Lexington, Mississippi, that worked for my wife's Aunt Gert. Just like me, Linda did not grow up around very many black people. So neither of us had any close black friends during our childhood or teenage years.

Linda actually had a black nanny herself, Miss Rosey. Both of her parents worked full-time jobs, so she spent a good deal of time with Rosey. She has always spoken of Rosey in an affectionate way, but her memories are devoid of any significant incidents involving race.

Florence had grandchildren that were around Linda's age. So whenever Linda would visit her aunt, she got to play with Florence's grandkids. Linda recalls a story from the 1950s when all of the kids decided to walk downtown to get some candy. Before the kids ever made it back home, someone had called Aunt Gert very upset. How dare she let a little white girl play and hang around with black kids?

When Linda and I were dating, we visited her Aunt Gert. Florence was still alive so Linda wanted to go see her. Several things caught my attention on that visit.

First, it was obvious that Florence was thrilled to see Linda. They smiled, hugged, laughed, and cut up. Second, several of the grandkids were there—the same ones Linda had played with as a child. They lived in Chicago now, but they were back home visiting their grandma.

They hated our guts.

I have no idea why. They were very terse and not at all subtle about their dislike of these two white people at their grandma's house. They were young adults, about our age.

As nice as it was to meet Florence, it was equally good to get out of there. I remember that I did not like being in a place where I felt disliked or unwanted.

At this point, I've given you most of the major experiences with black people that Linda and I had in our younger years. The reason I lay these out, is that we've had many black friends since that time. Even though we had almost no contact with black people growing up, we didn't continue on that path.

So I think it's interesting to note the progression, and find relevant clues as to how and why things change for the better. It's also interesting to note how our progress affects future generations by starting them off from a position that is much closer to the finish line of racial healing and harmony.

Learning to Value People

Right after graduating college and getting married, Linda and I moved to Hendersonville, North Carolina. The trip was long, and we had to take separate vehicles. I recall Linda being afraid to drive up Caesar's Head, a mountain in Western Carolina. That stretch of road capped off a long, winding two-lane highway, and Linda had never been to any mountains before, much less driven in the snow.

We spent our first night in Brevard, North Carolina, and sure enough, it snowed after we got settled in. The snow never bothered me, and Linda still swears she married a Yankee. That evening, I took Linda out for her first lesson on driving in the snow. The car decided to have a near miss with one of the telephone poles near our motel, so we ended our first snow-driving lesson very early.

The next day, I was to report to a DuPont plant in Brevard for my new job as a process engineer. We had planned for her to drive to Hendersonville so she could look for an apartment. There wasn't really any other option, so I told her, "Sweetie, you just get in the center of the road and go as slow as you need to go. If traffic backs up to Georgia, that's okay."

She got the job done.

Our apartment complex was relatively new and packed with young people. Many of the new graduate engineers hired by DuPont ended up living there. We were on the second floor, and the fellow living next to us was a young black engineer from Texas. His name was Ed, and he was a graduate of Prairie View A&M.

Ed worked for General Electric. I don't know if it was the physical proximity, the engineering connection, personal chemistry, or all of the above, but we really hit it off with Ed. He ended up becoming our best friend in Hendersonville.

At the time, Ed and I thought we were great tennis players, so we spent hours playing tennis and shooting the bull. He was our frequent dinner guest, and the three of us would often sit and talk for hours.

Ed was transferred to another location and two years later, Linda and I also left Hendersonville. We stayed in touch and when Ed met the love of his life—a precious lady named Juanita—we were honored to be invited to their wedding. Ed assured us we would not be the only white people there.

We were the only white people there.

It was totally fine though. Everyone made us feel like part of the family, especially Ed and his parents. Ed, Juanita, Linda, and myself have stayed connected. We remain friends nearly 50 years later.

As I write this, it is May 31st, 2020. George Floyd, an unarmed black man, was murdered this week by a white police officer in Minnesota. Juanita and Ed live in Minneapolis. We contacted them to see how they were doing. Juanita was at their winter home in Memphis, but Ed had stayed back to guard their home in Minneapolis.

After all these years, and as far as we have come together as a nation, I struggle to understand how this tragedy occurred. Was it driven by race? Did this white police officer see George Floyd as a life that was less valuable than other lives?

Had this police officer ever spent any time around black people? Did he ever have a black friend?

I don't know the answer, but I know that simply spending time with people of other races is one great way to cure many misconceptions or subconscious biases we may hold. If there was anything in my upbringing whatsoever that had planted any hint in my mind that somehow black people were defective, or less valuable, or not worthy of the fullness of human dignity, respect, and honor—well, that notion would have been obliterated simply by spending a little bit of time with wonderful people like Ed and Juanita.

The Sunset Gas Station

I started to do a chapter called "There are No Black People Here" but I thought it might give the wrong impression. The truth is, there are some parts of the United States where there are almost no black people. For instance, South Dakota currently has a black population percentage of 1.8%, and that's after a huge "explosion" of growth for the last 20 years. Obviously, it used to be pretty close to zero.

Beyond a few states with low black populations, the US is riddled with towns and counties that are historically white. We had a client one time in New Bremen, Ohio, and eons ago they were catching grief from federal officials because they did not have any black people working at their facility. Finally, in desperation, the company management responded to their critics, "I'll tell you what, if you can get some black people to move up here, we will hire them!" Obviously the people in DC had not taken demographics into account up until that point, because the response worked. They left them alone.

Linda and I were on vacation one year in the South Dakota and Wyoming area. We were having breakfast at a café and the waitress noticed Linda's University of Alabama sweatshirt. Somehow that made her want to talk about race relations.

She began enlightening us with her vast experience and knowledge (she was about 19 years old). After she had talked for a while, it was obvious to us that she had never seen a black person before. We figured out that she was talking about relations with Native Americans, because her points had nothing to do at all with Alabamians or black people.

She had been trying to connect with us on some level, and discuss how people of different races could get along with one another. But all the issues she mentioned were specific to Native Americans. We never mentioned to her that there are almost no Native Americans in Alabama. At some point in her life, she must have looked back on that conversation and laughed after figuring out the disconnect.

The point is, some people still to this day have scarcely seen or been around a black person. There are still some areas of the country that are nearly 100% white, or nearly 100% white + Hispanic, or nearly 100% white + Hispanic + Native American.

When that's the case, they really don't have any experience to go by. With little to no actual experience, it's easy to sit back and think the answers are all straightforward and simple. The answers to racial problems must seem obvious to anyone who isn't actually in the fray, living out their beliefs by walking through life with people of other races.

Speaking of places with very few black people, Western Carolina is one of them. The natural setting of Western Carolina is beautiful. They have some of the highest mountains east of the Mississippi River. That part of the United States was partly settled by prisoners from Europe—people who were either brought over as indentured servants, runaways, or people who had worked off their debt. Parts of Western Carolina fit the Appalachian stereotype of poor, rural, white mountain folks.

Lewis was a high school teacher who interned at our DuPont plant one summer. He was not just any old schoolteacher. Lewis was teacher of the year for the entire state of North Carolina. Being an intern in our process engineering group, Lewis stood out in several ways. He was not an engineer. He was older than most everyone else. He was black.

Our process engineering group was a close-knit group. Often we had to collaborate on projects, and we usually all at lunch together. Beyond that, DuPont had plenty of company and group activities on evenings and weekends. We all had a lot of fun together.

Lewis shared a story with us about coming down one of the mountains one time. He was trying to make it home and running low on gas. It was getting dark. He knew that a lot of the little mountain towns were "unfriendly to black people"—a gross understatement.

But he had to get some gas. As he pulled into the gas station, he noticed a handwritten sign out front: "[N-word], do not let the sun set on your a__ here."

As he pulled up to the pump, a burly white man met him immediately and said, "[N-word], can't you read?"

He promptly pulled back out and coasted most of the rest of the way down the mountain.

Lewis was a great human being. He did such an outstanding job at DuPont that they made him a full-time offer. North Carolina's loss became DuPont's gain.

In spite of being such an upstanding, productive member of society, Lewis had to endure things like the gas station episode—and who knows what else—throughout his life.

This is yet another one of those stories where I can't relate. Are there neighborhoods that are unfriendly to white people? Neighborhoods where I would stick out like a sore thumb, and perhaps invite trouble on myself merely by my presence? Yes, there are. But I generally don't have to drive through those places or stop in them.

Lewis didn't really have much of a choice. If he was going to live and function in society, he routinely had to face things like "the sunset gas station." It was just part of life for him. But he dealt with it and rose above it. Lewis was a good man, and I'm glad I had the chance to know him.

Pray for Black Men in America

After short stints in Mobile, Alabama, and Decatur, Georgia, Linda and I found ourselves living in Chattanooga, Tennessee, in the early 1980s. By that time, I was the vice-president of operations for a medium-sized paint manufacturer. Wherever we went, we always participated in the local chapter of the Alabama Alumni association.

Since there was not a chapter in Chattanooga at that time, Linda decided to start one up. She had learned that Ralph Stokes lived in Chattanooga. Ralph was a former Alabama football player under legendary coach Bear Bryant, and he had been on the 1973 national championship team. Linda figured if she could get Ralph to come on board as an engaged member, that would draw others in.

Ralph eagerly agreed to help. He said there were two organizations he would always support: The University of Alabama and the YMCA. He said both had made a huge impact on his life. Linda and I have no brothers or sisters, so that makes our friendships all the more special.

Ever since that time, Ralph and his wife, Debra, have been close friends of ours. If something had happened to us back then, our daughter would have gone to live with Ralph and Debra.

I'm not really sure why we became such good friends. The Stokes are just the kind of people that once you get to know them, you're friends forever. They're always on your prayer list, your mind, your heart. They're like family.

Beyond the fact that they're wonderful people, we also have a lot in common. We're all Alabama graduates. Besides football, Ralph ran track and played baseball. He's quite the golfer and currently serves as Director of Marketing for the PGA Tour Superstore. One time, he won a brand-new car by getting a hole in one during a golf tournament fundraiser. When he went to pick up the car, he saw that the dealership was having a drawing for a free vacation worth $10,000. Ralph won that too.

Anyway, while Ralph was the only elite athlete, all of us love sports. Beyond those connections, Ralph ended up working with us at Chesapeake Consulting for a time. We all have a deep faith in God. And finally, Debra is even more fun and interesting than Ralph.

The major lesson I draw from the success of our friendship with Ralph and Debra is that shared values are a major key. There has to be some kind of common ground, something that bonds you together. That's true for all relationships, but I think it's especially important for people of different races to have healthy, rewarding relationships.

Why is that? Probably because we have a lot of things telling us that we are different. Consciously or subconsciously, we've all been programmed to some degree to focus on differences among different races and cultures. Finding shared values is one way to overcome such programming or natural tendencies.

Several years back, Ralph gave me a call and wanted to know if I had seen the latest issue of Alabama Alumni Magazine. I had scanned it over, but had not noticed anything out of the ordinary. Ralph pointed out that the theme of the issue was the hope and future of the university. But there was not a single picture of a black person anywhere in the magazine.

Ralph was not particularly angry about this, but I could tell he was hurt. I listened as he vented his frustration.

After he hung up, I did feel anger begin to swell up inside of me. That is how it should work. Ralph is a loved one, and he was hurt. That made the issue personal for me.

I promptly popped the University President an email. At that time, I didn't mention Ralph's name, but I did express our shared dismay at this incredibly insensitive oversight. Within 15 minutes, the president had responded: "I will handle this—it will not happen again."

Later, I learned from a friend that the university president had called a meeting with the relevant parties to discuss the matter. He began the meeting by waving the magazine around in anger, letting everyone know exactly what the problem was. It never happened again.

Occasionally a blind hog will find an acorn. This is one of those opportunities in life where I somehow got it right. But it's important to note that my motivation was not to save the world. My motivation was not political. I wasn't trying to undo history or rectify the sins of the past. My friend was hurt, so I wanted to help fix it. It was personal to me.

"Pray for black men in America. It is a dangerous place for us." This is a text I received today, May 31st, 2020, from my friend Ralph. He's responding to the murder of George Floyd. He's hurt. My friend is hurt right now, and that makes it personal for me.

To every white man reading, and to myself, I say: We need to help fix this mess.

I don't have every answer, but I know we can start by listening more and talking less. We see things through a certain lens. People like my friend Ralph see it through a different lens. Have we really taken the time to listen to them? Have we taken time to understand their experiences? Their perspectives? Their feelings?

Those things matter.

Even if we find that we ultimately still disagree on many points, I think we will find that those feelings, perspectives, and experiences are real. And they matter.

I do not want our country to be a place where black men have to fear being murdered by police. I do not want our country to be a place where a white cop unloads his weapon on a 12-year-old boy playing with a toy gun (referring to the Tamir Rice incident, perhaps even more horrible than George Floyd's murder). I don't want our country to be a place where that same police officer not only doesn't get charged with murder, but actually gets to keep his job.

Something has to change, and it has to change now.

And it's going to change. The question is, how? Is it going to change through cooperation among people of all races, or is it going to change by some less peaceful method?

The choice is largely ours.

Change Doesn't Happen in Our Comfort Zone

One of the major ancillary benefits of being friends with a guy as lovable as Ralph is that you get to meet a lot of other really neat, wonderful people. Some of them have even become our friends. Pastor Kelvin Croom is one such man.

Kelvin is the younger brother of Sylvester Croom, the former head coach of Mississippi State University. Sylvester was the first black head football coach in the Southeastern Conference. He had also been an All-American football player at Alabama, and later played in the NFL. At Alabama, Sylvester had been in the same recruiting class as Ralph.

Sylvester and Kelvin's dad, Sylvester Sr., was possibly the most prominent black leader in central Alabama during the Civil Rights movement. He was also good friends with Bear Bryant. Sylvester Sr. had been an All-American football player himself at Alabama A&M, and later became a pastor. Clearly, these guys took after their dad.

During the spring of 2011, Tuscaloosa was hit by a series of devastating tornadoes, with the last one being beyond anything previously imagined. You can still find video of it today on YouTube, and it's absolutely massive. At times, it was a mile and a half wide, with winds of 190 miles per hour. Like I said, devastating.

The damage was severe. It ripped right through the middle of heavily populated areas, causing 64 deaths and more than 1500 injuries. At $2.1 billion, it also produced one of costliest cleanup and restoration bills on record for any tornado in United States history.

At the time, Linda and I were living in Maryland and we were both active in volunteering for missions work with our church. Linda organized two mission trips to Tuscaloosa. Members of the Severna Park United Methodist Church went down to help build new homes in the area.

Our crew of 25 would work during the day and then enjoy evenings however we wished. One Wednesday evening, Kelvin invited our group to join his congregation for worship. Kelvin's church, Collegedale Baptist, had been destroyed by the tornado and they were meeting in a temporary facility.

When we arrived, our little group was all white. I guess we had all sat down next to each other. Kelvin's congregation was all black. This apparently made for an unwelcome site from the pulpit because when Kelvin stood up, the first thing he said was, "I don't like what I'm seeing out there. I look over there, and it is all white. I look over on the other side, and it is all black. Everyone get up and move!"

Sometimes you just have to address the elephant in the room, even if it makes everyone uncomfortable.

From that time on, Kelvin and I have been friends, nearly ten years now. It's not unusual for him to call and lead us in prayer over the phone. I'm really glad he had the courage to say something that day, because it makes me realize that we just have to talk about things. We have to work through things. We have to talk about topics that are uncomfortable.

Kelvin is an important friend to me, who also happens to be black and to live in the same town. If I'm going to be intentional about working in my sphere of influence to improve race relations and to help fight injustice, it's going to be more important than ever for me to reach out to people like Kelvin and talk through uncomfortable topics with him. We'll have to be proactive about doing this, as such discussions rarely happen naturally.

Does that bring to mind anyone in your sphere of influence that you can reach out to? You don't have to set out to change the world. You can just set out to have a cup of coffee together, and see if there's anything you can change in *your* world. Your friendships. Your social gatherings. Your little league teams. Your PTA meetings.

Who can you reach out to? What needs to change? Are minorities being represented well? Do they have a voice? Are they made to feel welcome and comfortable? Find a way to reach out to local black leaders and ask what you can do to help correct racial injustice. I bet you they'll have some ideas.

Giving the Best to Our Children

About a decade ago, I was visiting my daughter, Leigh, in the hospital. Her friend Monica was in the room with us. Monica is a tall, slender black lady who could easily be on magazine covers as a model. She and Leigh had gone through a leadership program together and had obviously hit it off. Monica brought an enormous basket of goodies that day to give to Leigh. It was obvious to me that they adored each other.

To this day, Monica is still a fixture in the Covington family. When Linda cannot go to a football game with me, sometimes Monica is my "date." Whenever Monica has a boyfriend, we kindly request that they past muster with Linda, Leigh, and myself. She is part of our family, and I see that continuing forever. We just love her. It is fun having strong relationships with people.

Unlike Linda and me, Leigh grew up with parents who had black friends. It was not unusual to have black people in and out of our house regularly, whether they were midshipmen, just personal friends, or maybe people I worked with. Leigh went to a high school that was racially mixed, so she had several close black friends that she hung around with, including her cheerleader buddies.

She also had teachers, sports coaches, and other role models that were black. When she was little, her favorite babysitter was a local black girl who was also a cheerleader. When we lived in Chattanooga, there was a young black couple who lived across the street from us.

Both of them were medical doctors, and they had no children of their own yet, so they often played with Leigh.

Leigh also did club gymnastics growing up. Leigh actually competed against Dominique Dawes, a famous American Olympian gymnast. Leigh's gymnastics claim to fame is that she once beat Dominque in the vault. Leigh laughs that it was Dominique's worst ever performance on the vault, and Leigh's best ever. But still, pretty cool.

That story has nothing to do with race relations, but I appreciate you indulging this proud dad just a bit.

There is a relevant point to the mention of my daughter's gymnastics, however. Leigh's club met in Greenbelt, Maryland, and there were two black sisters on her team that Leigh became very good friends with. They would often spend the night with Leigh and vice versa.

Gymnastics parents often intermingle, so Linda and I ended up becoming friends with the girls' parents. They even stayed with Linda's dad one summer during a trip to Alabama for a gymnastics camp.

Now, before you decide that I'm just patting myself on the back for having positive interactions and relationships with black people, I do have an important point. This is different from the way I grew up. It's a lot different, and it's clear progress.

Given the way Leigh grew up, with close friends and role models who were black, it's unlikely that she would devalue black people in her mind and heart now that she's an adult. In fact, it's unfathomable to us in Leigh's particular case. But I'm trying to make a broader point here.

We must be proactive in pursuing and cultivating healthy relationships with people of other races. And we must involve our children in doing so as well. We all want to give the best to our children. Let's give them the best hearts and minds we can by teaching them to love, value, and pursue relationships with people of other races.

Doing so will change their lives for the good. But it's also one of the most important ways to bring about needed change in our society. As we interact with each other and learn to appreciate and value each other, the idea of one race somehow being less worthy than another naturally melts away.

The idea gets exposed for exactly what it is: insidious and stupid.

EIGHT

Your Assumptions Are Probably Wrong

For nearly four decades, I have taught leadership skills and how they impact the culture of an organization. Corporations, government entities, and organizations of all kinds actually pay me money to do this, and I consider myself blessed. Even though it always seemed to me like leadership gurus were a dime a dozen, I was always very passionate about the topic. So it never bothered me that there were so many 'experts' out there. I still felt obligated to throw in my two cents.

One critical teaching that I try to pass on is in regard to relationships. There are many good reasons—practical reasons—why an organization should encourage good relationships among its members. One of the main reasons is that information flows through relationships. If you want your sales department and your manufacturing department to communicate well, they need to know each other. They need to spend time together. They need to have good relationships.

In one of our workshops, I describe relationships as a pipeline connecting the brains of two people. Information flows through that pipeline. However, problems arise when odd beliefs begin to creep into the pipeline:

"All salespeople do is play golf, eat fancy dinners, and wear expensive shoes."

"Manufacturing people do not care about customer service."

"That guy is from New York, so he doesn't care about other people."

"That guy is from Alabama, so he probably has no clue what he's talking about."

These kinds of beliefs are basically plaque, crud, and refuse that build up in the pipeline, restricting the flow of information. And that's bad. Very bad.

Racial stereotypes fit into this category of beliefs.

The good news is that all of these assumptions are erroneous. And if we can purge them out of the pipeline, relationships will improve and information will flow.

Leadership is based on relationships. Relationships are based on trust. Trust is based on what we believe to be true. So we should constantly check what we believe to be true. We should explore what we actually believe and whether or not those beliefs are valid. The following are a few examples.

Chasing What Isn't There

Search and rescue dogs are trained to follow ground scents. One often used training exercise is to have a person walk through some area of woods or fields laying down a track. During this exercise, it's good for the person laying the track to leave a hot dog somewhere along the way in their footprint. The idea is to reward the dog for keeping their nose to the ground and following the scent.

Whenever the track layer makes a turn, they will put one of those small utility flags in the ground to indicate to the dog handler that a turn was made. After making the turn, the track layer normally puts down some extra hot dogs to reward the dog for finding the turn. Pretty quickly, the dog starts to associate those flags with extra hot dogs. Before too long, it becomes a firmly held belief. Utility flags = extra hot dogs.

Several years back, I was walking Maggie across the University of Alabama campus. A lot of construction was taking place and there were utility flags everywhere.

Maggie thought she had died and gone to doggie heaven. She rushes to the first group of flags, searching earnestly for the hot dogs. When she can't find anything, she turns her attention to the next group of flags. Still no hot dogs.

Finally, she comes to a point of recognizing that

utility flags do not necessarily equal extra hot dogs. In fact, they almost never indicate the presence of hot dogs. It only happens in one very specific time, place, and situation.

Maggie had her assumption invalidated. That's a good thing. When an assumption is wrong, it needs to be invalidated. Otherwise we spend our time in the wrong places, chasing the wrong things, and looking pretty stupid.

We All Have Biases

As I mentioned in the introduction, I have biases. I believe we all have them. The key is to keep them in check. Don't let them creep into our decision making or into our relationships. One of the things they teach at my church is: "Assume the best about people."

What a wonderful way to turn around the idea of bias. That concept works really well once you get into the habit of practicing it. All of your relationships and interactions with other people will improve if you can do that one thing. But most of us aren't there yet, at least not all the time. Most of us still struggle just to overcome the wrong negative assumptions we hold about other people and people groups. And yes, that includes stereotypes, assumptions, and biases we hold about people of different races.

About ten years ago, I was wrapping up a week spent in Wisconsin working with some clients. Wisconsin is one of those places with a heavily white population. In fact, the population is only about 6% black compared to 83% white.

After a great week of work, I was ready for a relaxing flight home. It was a Friday evening flight and weekend flights generally have a more relaxed feel to them. After making it through security, I found my gate and settled in with a nice book. I was looking forward to home.

Suddenly, my tranquility was interrupted. There was a guy next to me jabbering on his cell phone for the entire airport to hear. He was a black guy, dressed in very expensive designer clothes. But his clothes appeared to be about three sizes too big, and he also had a huge gold chain around his neck. He wore an expensive looking baseball cap with a flat brim. All of this seemed out of place to me for a guy who was well over 40.

Not only that, he had a beautiful woman sitting with him. She was dressed much more 'normal' and I thought to myself that this guy had surely outkicked his coverage. Was he some kind of rapper? A record producer? If so, what was he doing in Wisconsin?

Then a funny thing happened. As I overheard his conversation, I realized that this guy was a business owner. He was a contractor and he was lining up subcontractors for the next day's work.

Of all the people in the airport, I had more in common with this guy than anyone else. Immediately upon having this realization, I mentally kicked myself in the pants for being such a jerk. I had given in to a racial stereotype—an erroneous assumption.

We loaded the plane, and I had flown so much of late

that I was enjoying a free upgrade to first class. The seat next to me was empty so that was an even bigger bonus. My fellow businessman, the loud contractor with the odd clothes, was also in first class along with his beautiful wife.

Just as they were getting ready to cease boarding and close the airplane door, one more person enters—a young black man with wild looking hair. He was wearing very baggy clothes, a large gold necklace, and some kind of musical device plugged into his ears. He steps into the plane and looks around. Now keep in mind that I am an older, conservative-looking white guy who is dressed in business attire.

The young man immediately locks eyes on the empty seat next to me. He looked at me. I looked at him. And we both mentally said to ourselves, "Oh crap!" We had both planned for an enjoyable ride home, and now that wasn't going to happen. This guy was probably going to play loud music the whole time, be rude, or just generally annoy me somehow.

The young man appeared as distressed about his seat mate as I was. They closed the door and the plane began to taxi off from the gate. Being the old guy, I took responsibility to say the first words, feeling certain they would also be our last.

My assumptions were wrong again.

The young man turned out to be absolutely delightful. He was a college student at the University of Maryland who was working his way through school. He had been in Wisconsin visiting his girlfriend and he was intending to marry her soon. His plan was to start his own restaurant one day. We talked and talked. And then we talked some more. Before we knew it, we were landing in Maryland having thoroughly enjoyed each other's company.

In a period of about 20 minutes, I had let my bias go unchecked twice. It was only for a short time, but my goal is that negative bias would never go unchecked. Still, I am human. I am imperfect. If you're reading this, you are too.

What biases do you have that might need to be examined?

Why Do You Hate White People?

A few years back, some friends of ours had a son who was playing football for a major college football team. Shortly after a team victory, Linda and I were at a local bar having drinks with our friends. Their son, who was an offensive lineman, showed up and brought a lot of his friends. They were also on the football team.

All of the friends were white except for one black guy, who was a star running back. The running back was probably his closest friend. They began to relay a story of how one of their teammate's parents throws a party after each game, and everyone on the team is invited. But only the white players and their parents attend the party. None of the black players or their families ever come, we were told. There something dividing these guys along racial lines.

At that time, the star quarterback for the team was

black. He never came to these parties. This went on for about a year, and eventually the star quarterback ended up becoming roommates with the star running back. Since the star running back had close white friends, the quarterback ended up hanging out with some of them on occasion.

One day, our friend's son asked the quarterback bluntly, "Why do you hate white people? How come you never hang out with us or talk to us?"

The quarterback reacted with shock. "I thought you guys didn't like me! I beat out your white friend for the job, so I thought you guys didn't like me because of that."

"That is insane!" said my friends' son. "We're teammates. You're our quarterback. Of course we like you."

This story was sad to me. Neither of these young men had anything bad in their heart toward each other, except for assuming that the other was racist. Both of these young men had made a bad assumption about the other, and I'm willing to bet that any broader racial issue was based on an equally invalid assumption by one or more parties.

It's Not My Job to Fix Other People

"Dad, I am never, ever going to be nice to black people again. No more black friends! That's it!" This was the report from our daughter during her first semester in college. She can be a little dramatic at times. All of this odd behavior comes from her mother, as far as I know.

"Well how about the Stokes?" I asked.

"Well, they don't count. I can be nice to them," she conceded.

"How about Dolice?" I asked, referring to one of her cheerleader friends from high school.

"She doesn't count either," Leigh retorted.

I mentioned a couple of other black friends just to drive the point home and then asked, "Sweetie, you want to tell me what happened for you to come up with the revelation of no more contact with black people?"

She then proceeded to tell me about getting on an elevator in her dorm. Three black girls were already on the elevator. Once the door closed, they began to verbally assault Leigh with a barrage of racial epithets and vulgarity, venting anger on her that had absolutely nothing to do with her personally. They didn't know her at all. Her only crime, apparently, was being white.

The point I'm making here is that sometimes people actually do hate other people because of their race. These young girls apparently did hate Leigh just because she was white. And that can go in any direction. White people hating black people. Black people hating white people. And just about any other combination we can think of.

There is some crazy nonsense that gets paraded around as truth by many liberal, and so-called "politically correct" people. One of their recent ideas is that "black people cannot be racist."

That's complete baloney. Anyone of any race can be racist. We all know that. Those kinds of statements and ideas do absolutely nothing to promote racial harmony, and in fact, they do a lot to send it flying back in the other direction—toward disunity, anger, and division.

So I just wanted to acknowledge that truth because I know this is a sticking point with many white people. Yes, black people can also be racist. Most people who deny that are probably being intellectually dishonest. They probably have an agenda. I concede this point to any white guy out there who has this as a sticking point in his mind.

But while it's true that black people can be racist, that's really not my primary concern as a white person. As a white person, my primary concern is what I, and other white people, can do to help right wrongs. Correct injustice. Promote racial harmony.

Focusing on the handful of black people who are openly and strongly racist is the equivalent of getting in trouble for being late to class and then yelling back at the teacher, "But teacher, Tommy *skips class* all the time!" That kind of attitude and approach does nothing to help me. It does nothing to help me become the person I need to be so that I can be a positive, productive, and helpful member of society.

Focusing on the flaws of others is one way we try to avoid dealing with our own issues. It's not helpful.

NINE

What Can Us White Guys Do to Make Things Better?

Recall that I'm a Christian and therefore my views are from a Christian perspective. They are based on biblical teaching and insight. With that in mind, there are a few things I'd like to note. I think they will be helpful for anyone, Christian or not.

White supremacy, segregation, and all forms of racism are of the devil. Even if you don't believe in the devil, hopefully you acknowledge and understand the existence of evil. For Christians, we must recognize that this is spiritual warfare and we must approach it as such. The book of Ephesians has a great passage which explains the nature of these kinds of battles.

> *Put on the full armor of God so that you can fight against the devil's evil tricks. Our fight is not against people on earth but against the rulers and authorities and the powers of this world's darkness, against the spiritual powers of evil in the heavenly world. That is*

why you need to put on God's full armor. Then on the day of evil you will be able to stand strong. And when you have finished the whole fight, you will still be standing. So stand strong, with the belt of truth tied around your waist and the protection of right living on your chest. On your feet wear the Good News of peace to help you stand strong. And also use the shield of faith with which you can stop all the burning arrows of the Evil One. Accept God's salvation as your helmet, and take the sword of the Spirit, which is the word of God. Pray in the Spirit at all times with all kinds of prayers, asking for everything you need. To do this you must always be ready and never give up. Always pray for all God's people. (Ephesians 6:11-18 NCV)

There are evil supernatural forces behind racism. In other words, there are spirits of racism. Our war is not against human beings. There is an enemy that seeks to divide and conquer human beings. Just understanding this fact can often help bring much needed perspective to the conflicts we face in life.

Each one of us as individuals can primarily help fight and win this battle by improving ourselves. Once we can lead ourselves well, we can hopefully help bring others along with us. That's the very definition of leadership, after all.

Having studied and taught leadership principles for the majority of my life, I feel like I can sum up the majority of leadership with the following statement: People improve their leadership by improving their character (who they are) and by improving their intuition (what they know). Those are really the two main options for improving your leadership.

Improving What We Know About Racism

First, let's work on improving what you know—your intuition. Your knowledge base comes from one of three places:

(1) Your experiences

(2) Being taught directly by others

(3) Reading and studying others.

When it comes to knowing what it's like to be in the other person's shoes, we simply can't. We cannot experience life as a black person. It's not possible. But we can ask them about their experiences. We can listen with open minds and open hearts.

We can also read and study what prominent black voices have to say. I recommend doing so. Beyond that, it can be a helpful exercise to read people that you know for sure you strongly disagree with. That is definitely one way to challenge assumptions.

While preparing to write this book, I read a book called *White Fragility* by Robin DiAngelo. DiAngelo is white but she is very critical of white people. Her book was written in 2018 but enjoyed a popularity surge after the recent events surrounding the George Floyd murder. Please allow me to be frank.

DiAngelo's book stinks.

From what I gathered reading her book, she defines racism as being only something that is systematic, having even the power to impose laws. I call BS on that. Redefining terms is a form of manipulation. Racism is a term we've all used to mean something specific for a very long time, at least the last 50 years.

We've gotten to a point where probably 95% of the human population agrees that racism is wrong. Unjust. Evil, in fact. And now that we all agree racism is evil, people like DiAngelo want to change the definition and co-opt it to serve their agenda. They want to use the terms "racist" and "racism" as weapons. Basically, DiAngelo does what I mentioned before as being a recent trend. She labels all white people as racist while simultaneously declaring that it's not even possible for non-whites to be racist. How convenient.

Ms. DiAngelo is undoubtedly trying her best to do some good in the world, but I think she's going about it all wrong. Obviously, I find plenty to disagree with about Ms. DiAngelo's message.

But among all of her bashing of conservatives and white people, and her redefining of terms, she does put forth some useful information. What she's actually outlining is the concept of systemic racism. Systemic racism is much different from individual racism. A simple example would be Jim Crow laws.

It's possible that there might be an individual black

person who hated white people and would not allow them to vote, if given the power. If such a person did that, it would clearly be a case of individual racism. It should be noted that this sort of behavior would be labeled by DiAngelo only as "racial prejudice and discrimination." Somehow it wouldn't rise to meet the definition of "racism" in DiAngelo's view.

However, there have never been enough black people in the past to enact such laws against white people. But the opposite has been true. That's systemic racism, and it is a real thing. DiAngelo wants us all to redefine our terms so that systemic racism is the only thing that can be called "racism." If that were the case, one could confidently go around asserting that "black people can't be racist."

Again, we all know that's total nonsense.

But, it's true that black people in the United States have generally been the victims of systemic racism. White people generally have not. There were limited occurrences of serious discrimination against some white people in America's past. For example, Irish immigrants faced severe job discrimination,[1] and some were originally brought to the Americas as indentured servants.[2] Apparently, human beings have always been dumb. And evil.

But none of the discrimination faced by Irish immigrants was based on the color of their skin. Therefore, it was much easier for them to overcome the obstacles and assimilate. Much of the discrimination faced by black people was based completely on the color of their skin, and it was very institutional. They were dehumanized and denied basic rights. They were stripped of all human dignity. This treatment was systemic, and there are still vestiges of it that remain with us. This is all true. Ms. DiAngelo and I would probably agree on that, even though we may disagree about terminology.

Speaking of which, the term "white privilege" makes me cringe. The first problem is that it always seems to come from a liberal, and I must admit to being biased. It's hard for me to take liberals seriously. Immediately, anything they say is questioned and discounted in my mind.

However, looking back over my life and recalling many of the events described in this book, I have to admit that I was never disadvantaged because of my race. Like the vast majority of white people in America, I had to work very hard for everything I have and everything I've accomplished. That's true for most Americans—roughly 4 out of 5 have never received any kind of inheritance.[3] The average American will inherit very little in their lifetime, and if they get anything at all, it will probably come very late in life. In fact, we're just as likely to have to shell out a lot of money directly, and in the form of lost wages, taking care of our elderly parents.[4]

There is a lot of misperception in America. Even the vast majority of wealthy people earned their wealth, rather than inheriting it. But for some reason, that isn't what the average person believes. A recent study found that 74% of millennials "believe millionaires inherited their money." 52% of baby boomers believe the same. But the actual numbers are this: Only 21% of millionaires received any inheritance at all. Only 3% of them inherited a million dollars or more.[5]

Studies also show that people who have earned their wealth through working tend to feel that their kids should do the same.[6] Many of them donate a large part of their wealth. Bottom line, the idea of generational wealth and privilege being the norm for white people just isn't so.

So here is the truth, and this is why most of us white people get upset at the term "white privilege." I worked for everything I have. No one ever gave me any award for being white. No one ever gave me a job because I was white. No one ever handed me any money or resources because I was white.

But no one ever kept me from opportunities because I was white, either. I didn't have to leave the Naval Academy after being terrorized because of my race. If anything, my race has benefited me. It certainly has not caused me any disadvantage or obstacles in our society. For the most part, my black friends cannot say the same.

Still, I don't like the term "white privilege" and I do not intend to use it. I think some people use the term to denigrate white people and invoke guilt on them, and I don't want to join in that. I also don't think use of the term does anything to lead to racial unity, harmony, and healing. But I certainly understand the concept. If some of my liberal friends choose to use the term, I am resolved that I won't be offended or react in a hostile way to them using the phrase.

Semantics and negative connotations aside, I think most of us can agree that black people have faced many obstacles and challenges that white people have not faced. So I would just say to my fellow white men that even though we may not like the term "white privilege" we can acknowledge the difficulties black people have faced and still face in this country. And we can work to help correct those problems.

We get mad and shake our fist at things like "affirmative action" because it comes through the heavy hand of government. But what if we just decided to help correct the problem without any coercion whatsoever? What if we just decide that we're going to personally work to help set things right? What if we go out of our way to help, hire, promote, build, advance, and encourage young black people? What if we went out of our way to help provide them opportunities? No government coercion should be needed for us to do that.

Let me stop here and acknowledge that many people and companies are doing those very things. Diversity goals and targets have become a major focus for most large corporations over the last 30 years. But I'm really trying to speak here to each individual. I'm trying to speak to what's in our hearts toward our fellow man. Hiring more black people to appease critics and ease political pressure is one thing. Doing it because we actually care about what they've gone through, and we want to help correct injustice whenever and however we can—now that makes God smile.

The first step is to acknowledge that being black in

the United States is a lot different from being white. You and I, my white friends, do not put a high priority on our race as part of our personal identity. We almost never even think about it. But our black friends do. For them, color is close to a nerve—something that is very important and sensitive—and with good reason.

We just haven't experienced the kinds of things they have personally experienced. We also haven't been told by our parents and grandparents about all the horrible things they suffered due to their race. We don't have that history, so it is difficult for us to empathize. But we can listen and learn and try to understand them. In that spirit, here are a few more responses from my black friends when they were asked this question:

"If you could snap your fingers and make it happen, what would you want white men to understand about racism?"

- *That racism is real and continues to exist and no amount of ignoring it or claiming to be "color blind" is going to change that reality.*

- *It starts at home in the subtlest of ways. It is often formed out of an accumulation of tiny slights, rejections, offenses, and other forms of direct or perceived indignations over a period of time.*

- *It begins with the celebration of one group or*

person's characteristics at the expense of another's—somehow ascribing those, in a generic way, to all who look like that person.

- *We stereotype, sometimes out of humor, other times out of judgment, or anger, or frustration. But regardless, we begin to share those thoughts out loud, opine on them, and act on them. All the while, we subtly begin setting the example for our families that these conclusions and actions are right and justified. We perpetuate the vicious cycle, even if we do so unknowingly, through unconscious bias.*

- *Never say that racism doesn't exist, or that it isn't systematic. Try proving it is not.*

- *If you are a Christ-follower, you are called to love everybody and that takes intentionality.*

- *Not all black people think the same. No one black person can speak for the entire group.*

- *White privilege is real.*

- *As an American who happens to be of African descent, I have paid my dues in every way to this—my country—through service to it and to mankind. It is not different from that which you have done and for the same reasons—pride of ownership! I am proud of this country and all that it entails as well as to call it my own; therefore, there is no wish list for me as a Black man or as an American. My expectations are as high as the sky is above for me and my family.*

- *We never healed as a country after Reconstruction and never made Black Americans whole and fully a part of the American experiment.*

- *My parents trained me to never go into a store unless I intended to purchase something and to keep my hands out of my pockets. Also, to make sure I got a receipt.*

- *No one is asking you to riot or sit-in someplace, or to picket a business. But you can begin reaching out, on a human level, to your co-workers or neighbors, or someone who looks entirely different than you. You can offer your regrets at whatever indignity they may have endured because of their difference, and you can offer to help.*

Black Lives Matter

When people say "Black lives matter!" what they're really saying is "Black lives matter too!" Black lives matter just as much as other people's lives. And they are inviting all of us—challenging us—to show that we believe it too.[7]

For us to come back and say "all lives matter" is hurtful at best. That response discounts and denigrates their message. I would like to challenge you just a bit to stop and think for a moment.

My next-door neighbor, Sam Woodward, gave one of the best analogies I have ever heard about the common use of this phrase. Here it is:

Imagine a cookout where all of the neighbors are invited. Everyone is seated outside at round tables. The hostess, Karen, brings everyone steaks and sides. Mashed potatoes. Gravy. Macaroni and cheese. The food is great. Everyone is enjoying it and having their fill—except Joe, that is.

Joe hasn't been served.

Pretty soon Joe says, "Hey, where's my steak? I'm hungry."

Karen responds, "Everyone is hungry, Joe. Stop complaining."

Karen is technically correct. Everyone is hungry. But everyone else is being taken care of, while Joe is left out.

How does all of this apply to you personally? Well, let's think through some scenarios and find out.

Let's say that you hear on the news that a promising young college student ruined his own life by getting completely wasted and committing some terrible crime in the process. He had been an honor student, and this was totally out of character for him. He got drunk and burned down a building. Now instead of graduating college in the spring, he will be in prison for arson.

Does that story bother you?

It bothers me. What a terrible waste of life. I imagine it bothers you too.

Now, let's say that in the midst of watching this news story, they flash a video of the young man. He's about 6 foot 5 inches tall, and very muscular. He has wild dreadlocks and a long bushy beard. He wears the latest Kanye West gear, diamond earrings, and several gold chains. And he's black.

Does that ease the pain you feel? Does it somehow seem "not quite as tragic" now? Try to be honest with yourself here.

Let's imagine this same scenario but the young man is white. He's of average height and build. He's dressed in a blue blazer and tan slacks. His upper middle-class white parents are in the background sobbing, and pleading for leniency for their son. They lament how he could have ever fallen into this. He's such a good kid. They want you to look at all the good things he's done, and not judge him based on this one single act.

Do those scenarios feel different in any way at all to you? How do you think the average jury might assess those situations differently, especially if the hypothetical jury was mostly white?

Let's take it a step further. Picture this scenario. You get an AMBER alert on your phone. A 3-year-old girl was just kidnapped, and it happened in your town! The mother was the victim of a carjacking and the little girl was asleep in the back seat. Horrible!

You start to pray for the little girl and her mother. You go to social media and see what you might be able to do. Maybe you can raise awareness. Maybe you can keep an eye out for the vehicle.

As you start to research, you find out where the carjacking happened. It was over in the bad area of town. The little's girl's name was Kiara. Her mom's name was LaKiesha. You find a few pictures of them. They were clearly very poor.

Does your sense of urgency and injustice and horror diminish a little bit? You were picturing a nice, middle-class white family getting carjacked. And their daughter was kidnapped in the process. Oh the injustice! Oh the horror that poor mom must be feeling!

But now that you know it's a little black girl from the opposite side of town, does it feel less tragic? I can't answer that question for you. I just want you to consider it.

Let's say a 12-year-old boy has gotten a new toy gun

from his parents. He takes it up the street to a local park and he's just out playing and having fun. Doing what little boys do.

All of a sudden, a local policeman jumps out of his vehicle with his weapon drawn. Within 20 seconds, he has riddled this little boy's body with bullets. That one actually happened in 2015. If you're not already familiar with it, please look up the case of Tamir Rice.

It happened, and we all dropped the ball on that one. Not only did the white police officer not get charged with murder, he actually got to keep his job. Shocking.

Can you imagine the outcry from white people if this had happened in a suburb? To a little white boy?

It's probably human nature to empathize more with the people who look like us. But if so, that's part of our *sinful* human nature. God has given us the capacity to choose good over evil, even though we are most often predisposed toward evil and selfishness.

This tendency to place less value on the life of a black person, or anyone who doesn't look like us, is something we must work to overcome. For the last 30 years or so, I have watched as the vast majority of white people defended police nearly every time there was some questionable shooting, beating, or mistreatment of a black person caught on video.

"Police put their lives on the line every day. We don't know what they deal with. We don't know what it's like to be in their shoes."

"We didn't see what happened before the video started rolling."

"If the police tell you to get on the ground, just get on the ground."

"The suspect had a criminal record! Case closed!"

What has looked very open and shut to many of us white people is not quite so open and shut. Normally when we see the police, we feel more safe. We believe they are there to help us. To protect us.

Many black people do not have those same feelings. If a policeman tells a black man to get on the ground, that black man might very well be thinking, "Why? So you can shoot me in the back of the head?"

Or maybe now, they're thinking, "Why? So you can put your knee on my neck and choke me to death? I don't think so."

This has to change.

Black lives matter.

Period.

Improving Your Character

Every human being is made up of three parts.

(1) Your body – this is the physical part of you.

(2) Your soul – where your mind resides, your emotions, your will.

(3) Your spirit – this is the eternal part of you. The part that has its origin in a different realm.

The Bible teaches that we all have a spirit. However, it is considered "dead" unless and until we receive Christ as Savior. Then the Holy Spirit raises our dead spirit to life, which is the meaning of the phrase "born again." We are born a second time, this time of the Spirit.

Human beings are made in the image of God, and this is one way we reflect his image. He is a three-part being: Father, Son, and Holy Spirit. And we are three-part beings: spirit, soul, and body.

One of those three parts is going to run the show for us. Both the body and the soul crave. The longer they go without sustenance, the more they crave. The body says things like, "I am hungry. Feed me." The soul says, "You hurt my feelings. You must apologize to me."

If you do not feed your spirit, it will not crave. Your spirit simply won't show up. It will let you go your own way.

Here's the key point: we cannot solve a spiritual problem if we do not engage the spirit. Remember that this is spiritual warfare, and we cannot go into battle unarmed.

Isaiah 11:2 states:

"The Spirit of the Lord will rest on him—the Spirit of wisdom and of understanding, the Spirit of counsel and of might, the Spirit of the knowledge and fear of the Lord."

Daily I ask for the Holy Spirit's help. Here is what I

pray, which is from a prayer booklet provided by Church of the Highlands:

> *"Holy Spirit, I ask You to fill me up. I need Your presence in my life, guiding, directing, comforting, and counseling me. I know that You, Holy Spirit, are God, in the Trinity with God the Father and the Son, Jesus. You are the Spirit of Wisdom, Understanding, Counsel, Might, and Knowledge. Give me a holy fear of the Lord, helping me to be in awe of who God is and what God does. Work in me, Holy Spirit. Teach and transform me (pray through any areas where you feel the need for transformation today). I honor You and ask You to empower me with Your spiritual gifts for the good of the church."*

When the Holy Spirit works in us, the Bible tells us what the result will be:

> *"But the Holy Spirit produces this kind of fruit in our lives: love, joy, peace, patience, kindness, goodness, faithfulness, gentleness, and self-control. There is no law against these things!"* (Galatians 5:22-23 NLT)

Max Lucado, a wonderful Christian pastor, author, and theologian, has written out a set of declarations based on the nine fruits of the Spirit.[8] He starts with the first one by saying, "I choose love. No occasion justifies hatred; no injustice warrants bitterness. I choose love. Today I will love God and what God loves." And then there is a similar declaration for each fruit of the Spirit. I read and pray through Lucado's declarations three times a week so that I can internalize them.

What I'd like to do here is adapt the concept and offer a similar set of declarations that us white guys can use to help us fight against racism.

I will love God and love others. Since God loves everyone, I will love everyone.

The guy who has his pants hanging down below his rear end? God loves him. The fellow talking in a way that is not making any sense to you? God loves him. It is a lot easier to love the black man who seems a lot like me— middle class or upper middle class. But I am to love everyone.

I choose to share joy with all human beings, regardless of their race. I will delight in the opportunity to interact with people of all races.

This one makes me think of my interactions with the guys at Bibb County Correctional Facility in Brent, Alabama. I'm blessed to be part of a group that gets to go in and hold church services there. During these meetings, there are no racial lines or racial divides. Black, white, and Hispanic men are all filled with joy to see each other and worship together.

I choose to walk in peace with my fellow man, even if they hurt or offend me. I will not hold an entire race of people responsible for the actions of a few.

My daughter was treated rudely by some college girls in her dorm. They were black. Linda and I were treated rudely by the grandchildren of her nanny. They were black. It would be insane for us to somehow hold this against all black people. In fact, it would be detrimental to hold the offense against anyone at all. As my pastor often says, "Walking in unforgiveness is like taking poison and waiting for the other person to die."

Maybe you've been mistreated by someone of another race. Maybe you are tired of the media and social media blaming all problems on white people.

Can you overlook the offense, and choose to forgive? Forgiveness does not mean condoning the behavior. It simply means "letting go."

I choose to be patient with people who look, sound, or interact in a way that is different from what I'm used to.

Some people don't have the same social norms that I have. They may talk or interact with me in ways that I find annoying. But for them, maybe it's not annoying at all. Maybe that's just the way they typically interact. I can choose to be patient when I find myself in those situations.

I choose to practice kindness toward people of other races.

We all hear about random acts of kindness. There's a funny thing about that: acts of kindness are much more likely to happen if we plan them. We have to be intentional. Think of a black person you know or have seen and figure out a way to do something kind for them. Maybe you know someone who could use a business connection or an introduction to a hiring manager. Whatever the case may be, just do it without wanting anything in return.

I choose goodness toward people of other races.

What came to my mind for this one was to intentionally look for ways to highlight the achievements of black co-workers. Not in a patronizing or insincere way. This is something we would do for anyone we like and are friends with. We look for ways to build them up, promote them, and bless them. But maybe there is a person of another race in your workplace, and you don't know them that well, so you've never felt comfortable publicly honoring them. Step out of your comfort zone. Get it done.

I choose to be faithful toward people of other races.

Do you include people of other races in opportunities, events, and social gatherings? All it takes is a little intentionality. Sometimes people slight other people without consciously intending to do that. There are certain people in our lives that we just honestly forget to reach out to or include. We need to dig deep and ask ourselves whether we've done that with people of other races, and then work to correct the problem.

I choose to be gentle toward all people, yet simultaneously bold in building them up through loving correction.

We have a men's leadership breakfast that meets most Wednesday mornings. One of the things we do is talk about our weaknesses. Loving help and correction is crucial to everyone's development. It's part of teaching and training people. It would be unloving if we withheld such correction from people of other races just because we're afraid of hurting their feelings. But we can be gentle as we give our friends feedback.

As a white man, it is not my place to correct my black friends on issues involving race. It just isn't my place. But I can help them in other areas, and I can do so in a loving way.

I choose self-control in regard to race relations.

If you are with your white friends and someone makes an insensitive racial comment, do you have enough self-control to do the right thing? Or do you shy away in fear of being "that guy" to your friends?

What about your own comments? Your social media posts? Are they insensitive to people of other races? We may really want to hit that share button, but we need to pause. Pray. Ask the Holy Spirit: Is this good, lovely, excellent, and praiseworthy? Is it helpful? Good? Holy?

If not, I will exercise self-control. I will hit the delete button instead.

Be Proactive in Developing Relationships with Black People

Distance does not make the heart grow fonder. We're all familiar with the form of segregation that was condoned by governments and organizations. We agree that it was evil and wrong. But do we believe it is evil when it happens by preference?

We cannot build relationships without trust. It's tough to build trust between people who never get together for some kind of unified reason. From 1985-2015, we lived in an upper middle-class neighborhood in Maryland. It was a large community with somewhere around a thousand homes. Possibly ten of those homes housed black families, and it may have been less than that.

During that same period, we went to a church which averaged about 300 people on a Sunday morning. There might be two black people there on any given Sunday, and one of them was the wife of a church official.

I used to see black people at work when I was with Sherwin-Williams. We might also encounter black people when attending some regional church meeting or training. Our friendships with black people seemed more limited in Maryland, even though the statewide black population is above 30%.

As I mentioned previously, we did have interactions with black people whenever possible. We had black dinner guests and midshipmen in our home, and my daughter had black friends. So my family and I made black friends in Maryland, but it was not as easy there. I think it was due to less opportunities.

If you can believe this, we have actually found that there is less segregation in the south.[9]

Back in Chattanooga, our neighborhood had been a little more racially diverse, with maybe 10% black families. Again, it was an upper-middle class neighborhood and we lived there from 1980-1985. We had met Ralph and Debra Stokes during that time, and they had become lifetime friends. So we found that we had more success building close relationships with black people in Tennessee than in Maryland.

Now, it's not necessarily my intent to lift Alabama as a beacon of race relations. But strangely enough, we've had a much better experience here than anywhere else. I see several reasons for that:

(1) *In our upper-middle class neighborhood in Alabama, the population is at least 40% black.* Most everyone in our neighborhood has a college degree. Our first close neighbor was Wendell Hudson. A retired basketball player, Wendell was the first ever

black athlete on scholarship at the University of Alabama. He was also the head coach of the women's basketball team at UA for a time. We naturally became friends because we lived next door to each other. That just didn't happen in Maryland.

It's the same with other people. When I go on walks in the morning in my neighborhood, I have a lot of conversations with neighbors. Forty percent of them are black, so naturally that makes it much easier to develop black friendships. Linda is active in our homeowner's association and her best buddy there is a black lady named Sherry. They like to decorate the neighborhood together on special occasions and holidays.

(2) *The University of Alabama has been a leader in just about every category of racial diversity for decades now.* I'm blessed to be able to serve on several boards connected with the university. Many of the people I serve with, and those we serve, are black. UA is not perfect by any stretch and we cover some of the more glaring mistakes in this book. But there are generally very good relations between blacks and whites here.

(3) *In general, the community here is better connected across races.* We will discuss this more in the section on government, but here I will note that when I go to community meetings for leaders in Alabama, it's generally much more racially diverse than any other place I've been.

(4) *Many of the churches here are integrated.* We are members of the largest church in Alabama, a multi-site megachurch. It's also the second largest church in America. People of all races attend, and the percentages of each race reflect the general population.

Again, no place is perfect. So what have I noticed here that needs work? For starters, in some parts of town the public school system is not perceived as being good. Some of them are essentially segregated.

For instance, Central High School downtown is nearly 100% black, a situation which reflects the reality of the surrounding neighborhoods. Bryant High School is 87% black. Our neighborhood is zoned for Bryant. I've noticed that most of the families in my neighborhood—white or black—who have school aged children send them to private schools.

So we still have work to do in Alabama, but generally, we've had much more success here developing relationships with black people. There seems to be more connectedness across races than in other places we've lived.

No matter where we live, progress requires intentionality. Having good friends requires hard work and intentionality. No matter who they are or what color they are, relationships take effort. We're all busy, and it's hard to keep up with other people, especially the way most of us move around now due to our careers. So most people do not put building relationships high on their priority list.

Let's not be like most people.

When we write things down, they have an 85% better chance of happening than when we don't write them down. I find that using a piece of paper is better for me, as things seem to get lost easier inside an electronic device. Bottom line, put it on your to-do list: I will work at building friendships with people of other races.

TEN

Try Not to Do Anything Stupid

It is my understanding that medical doctors' first and primary call is to "do no harm."

My white friends, we need to take a page out of their playbook. Let's commit ourselves to "do no harm" by not saying or doing anything stupid. What do I mean by this? The kind of stupid I'm referring to is best illustrated with a few recent examples. These stories hit the newswires in the middle of me writing this book.

(1) In 2019, three black gymnasts from the University of Alabama team were all working on the vault during practice. They were laughing amongst themselves that all of the black girls wound up on the vault at the same time. A white male assistant coach walks up and says, "What is this, the back of the bus?"[1] This is just my personal guess, but I think this coach probably walked up on a conversation that

made him feel out of place and uncomfortable. He reacted by saying something really dumb. Silence is always an option in uncomfortable or out of place situations. To his credit, the coach seems to have turned away from this behavior and also issued a heartfelt apology, basically saying, in so many words, that he never intended to hurt anyone. He just said something really dumb.

(2) The University of Alabama gymnastics head coach was also accused of saying the following about one of her black assistant coaches: "She's not really black. She wasn't really raised black."[2] What does that even mean? I don't know if she actually said that or not. But if she did. Stupid.

(3) One of the other allegations involved white gymnasts using the "n word." It's shocking that this is still an issue, but it is. In modern times, it's well known that some black people have appropriated the use of that word, turning it back as a "popular term of endearment," according to Professor Neal A. Lester.[3] What was a symbol of hate and oppression, they turn around and use in a different way. But I want to be as clear as possible to every white person out there: They can use it. You can't. The end.

A lot of stupid things come about from someone trying to be cute or funny. If you are not currently getting paid to be a comedian, resist the temptation to be one—especially with anything even remotely connected to race. Just don't do it.

Another thing that just never comes across well is when us white people try to prove that we aren't racist. For example, pointing to the fact that we have black friends. Or maybe pointing out that we donate money that somehow benefits black people.

When we say these things as a way to show that we aren't racist, we reek of defensiveness. Everybody else can see it, and it just never comes across well. Your black friends might be polite and not say anything negative back to you, but trust me. They don't want to hear these kinds of comments. They come across as patronizing at best.

In her book, DiAngelo actually covers a list of supposed "evidence" white people often give to show that they aren't racist. While I haven't actually heard most of the reasons in DiAngelo's list given during real life conversations, I think they are generally indicative of the tendencies we have to defend ourselves in this area. For that reason, I found them useful. And I have actually heard some of them in real life. The list is on pages 77 and 78 of her paperback, should you want to check them out.

So what *can* you say?

After reading the last few paragraphs of this book, you might be feeling like you can't do anything right in regard to race relations. Here's the key: we're talking here about everyday, casual conversations and interactions with people. I do encourage you to get to know people of other races on a deep, personal level. I encourage you to discuss difficult issues. When you do, something might come across in a way you didn't intend. That's part of working through messy topics.

But to my fellow white men, I need to say this, and please hear my heart. We should be doing a lot more listening, and a lot less talking when it comes to matters of race. So when you have those deep, meaningful discussions with your black friends—either prompted by them or after asking their permission to discuss racial issues—be a student.

Listen.

Learn.

And when it comes to those everyday, casual interactions with people of other races, remember that silence is golden. You don't have to try to tackle the latest racial issues of the day in your office small talk. And in casual conversation especially, you don't have to defend yourself as not being a racist.

Just don't be one.

Don't Get Caught Up in Every Battle

As I mentioned previously, I am writing this book in early summer of 2020. Hopefully, we are nearing the end of the coronavirus scare, although there is still plenty of anxiety about a possible "second wave." Beyond that, we are only several months from the general elections, and emotions are running high across the board. The murder of George Floyd is still very fresh in everyone's mind and heart.

During this kind of turmoil, there are plenty of good, spiritual people who have their words and actions in alignment with God's heart. However, the devil also uses people to achieve his goals. Again, I would remind us to be aware of the spiritual battle taking place, and use sound judgment before involving ourselves in controversy.

Many years ago, I had a friend refer me to a Bible verse that can help us deal with all the divisive rhetoric being disseminated over the airwaves.

> *"The people of Berea were more open-minded than the people of Thessalonica. They were very willing to receive God's message, and every day they carefully examined the Scriptures to see if what Paul said was true." (Acts 17:11 GWT)*

We can do the same today with each message that comes our way. We can ask, does it align with God's Word? Is there something here that I need to do? If yes, by all means, go and do it. If not, block out the message and press on towards the goal of unity.

ELEVEN

Working through Our Churches

"I do not have to put up with this crap!" I fumed to myself after driving off from a black church in Maryland, in 1992. "This class is far enough along. The other teachers can finish it off. They do not need me."

It was right after the LA riots. The riots occurred after four white officers were acquitted of all charges. The officers had severely beaten Rodney King, a black motorist. The whole thing was caught on video, so it's still a wonder how they were acquitted. It was a savage beating that went on for a long time.

The riots further inflamed racial tensions, especially after black rioters pulled a white truck driver from his vehicle and beat him nearly to death. There was a lot of tension in the air for everyone, regardless of race.

While teaching the Bible study that evening in the church, I was the only white person present. The Bible study had gotten very heated and harsh words were hurled at me. There was a young black lady who was especially angry. We'll call her Sharon. Sharon was in her 20s or 30s. My response was not one of anger, but I was tired of putting up with criticism. I didn't feel that I deserved any of it. As much as I loved the members of my class, I felt that they would do just fine without me there.

The irony is that this Bible study was conceived and enacted to establish better race relations. Some pastors had gotten together, and with the best of intentions, decided it would be good to get the members of our all white church together with the members of an all black church nearby.

The Bible study was an intense 36-week program. The class met once a week for nearly three hours. By the end, we would have gone through 80% of the Bible together. We took prayer requests and prayed for each other, got to know each other, and we learned together. Prior to the Rodney King jury verdict, we had made it through the better part of the course, and we were all getting along very well.

The way things worked in our denomination was that to teach this class, you must have previously co-led the class along with a lead instructor. I was the lead instructor, and I had two black co-leaders from the church. They were in the training period to be able to teach the class on their own going forward.

So I had sat at a stoplight fuming about all of this. As the light turned green, and I pulled off, I sense a little tap on my shoulder. A familiar voice came into my mind. "Oh no you don't. You certainly do have to put up with that crap. I expect you to finish the course with them."

"Huh?" I wondered to myself. "Was that the voice of the Holy Spirit? Does God use the word 'crap'?"

Rather than risk getting hit with a bolt of lightning, I decided to finish the semester. But going back the next week wasn't going to be fun. I dreaded it.

Fast forward a few years later. I was at a high school basketball game and I heard someone yelling my name. There she was. The young lady who had been so angry in 1992, reaching out to me for a big hug. Sharon and I hugged and hugged, and then caught up with each other. She filled me in on how many of our former class members were doing. One of my co-instructors was about to get ordained as a minister, which made me feel proud and happy for him.

Sharon and I ended up seeing each other frequently in the area over the coming years, and I got lots and lots of hugs. I still love this lady today. She is my friend and I feel a deep sense of connection to her.

None of that would have happened if those pastors hadn't gotten together and been intentional. They knew it wouldn't be easy or comfortable for everyone, but they decided to get our congregations together. Besides that, the rest of us had to be intentional about working through difficult issues. We had to persevere when it got uncomfortable. Tough. Heated.

There must be an intentional effort among the faith community to connect people of different races.

While there is some diversity among the traditional denominations and sects of Christianity, a lot of churches are still largely segregated. The most diversity I have personally witnessed has always been in relatively new, non-denominational churches. And those churches are growing and spreading like wildfire.

If you are a pastor, you might want to seriously consider rocking the boat a little in this area. Anytime you change something at older, tradition-driven churches, there will be long time members who leave.

And your church is normally a lot better off without them.

Don't worry about the economic impact of a few tithers leaving. God is your provider. As a pastor or other church leader, you're not supposed to be catering to people because of what they can do for you economically or socially—at least not according to the Bible.

> *If you show special attention to the man wearing fine clothes and say, "Here's a good seat for you," but say to the poor man, "You stand there" or "Sit on the floor by my feet," have you not discriminated among yourselves and become judges with evil thoughts? (James 2:3-4 NIV)*

There's that word again: evil. If anyone opposes efforts to racially integrate your church, there is certainly a spiritual warfare issue happening. Such opposition definitely doesn't come from God.

While church leadership and church trends are not among my areas of expertise, I see two basic models of church emerging in the 21st century.

First, there is the traditional denomination or single

church model. These are mostly small and medium sized churches that operate largely independent of each other, even though they may be under the umbrella of a bigger organization. Typically, this type of church is less racially diverse. A lot of intentionality is required here. Here are three possible ways to help remedy the segregation problem that exists:

(1) Merge. Businesses merge. Governments merge. Churches can merge. Mostly white congregations can get together with mostly black congregations and simply decide to merge. Prove me wrong.

(2) Do Bible studies, mission trips, and community projects together. Do them often, and stay the course.

(3) Seriously pray and consider joining a mostly black church. I wouldn't advise just walking in one day and announcing that as part of an effort to improve race relations, you're there to join the church. But I would advise seriously praying about the issue and then going and talking to the pastor of a mostly-black or all-black church. Share your heart with him, and ask if it's something he would welcome. Just explore the idea together. See what happens.

The second basic church model is the non-denominational, multi-campus megachurch. These probably still account for a small percentage of the total church going population. But the growth rate is high, and many more are being planted. As of right now, they appear to be the way of the future.

Most of these types of churches do not seem to have much of a diversity problem. Still, they should be intentional about ensuring that their governance and leadership structure reflects the diversity of their congregation.

Small Groups

Small groups are a great way for churches to help build positive relationships among people of various races. Having been involved in many small groups at my current church, I can honestly say that it's very difficult to come away from them feeling anything but brotherly love and a sense of connection with the other group members.

Once a small group system is instituted, everyone involved should stay aware and be proactive on the issue of diversity. Currently, I'm attending a small group known as the "Men's Leadership Breakfast." We meet together early mornings on Wednesday and discuss leadership podcasts. Because our church is fairly well integrated, we typically don't have to go out of our way to try to integrate our small groups.

But for this particular leadership group, I noticed that our membership was consistently running 100% white males. We *did* have to go out of our way to start inviting black friends. We have to practice awareness of this issue because naturally, we may not even notice when we're sitting in a room with a bunch of other white males. That is, until a black person shows up to one of our meetings. Then we may all start to notice the diversity issue, especially if the new member doesn't know anyone else before they get there. The bottom line is we want all people to feel welcomed and comfortable in every setting, so let's be proactive in reaching out to people of other races.

Another small group I'm involved in is predominantly made up of older men. To be more precise, the group is all men in their 50s and 60s and 70s, except for one younger man in his 30s. One day, I looked around and said, "Micah, what are you doing in this group with a bunch of old guys?"

He responded, "John, I can't learn anything hanging out with a bunch of guys my age." He was intentional about joining a group that was made up of older men so that he could learn more. That's great wisdom and we can apply it to our small group systems in more ways than one. The group itself will learn more and be more robust if we are intentional about diversity.

TWELVE

Being Active in Government

"Let us bow our heads for a word of prayer."

I was taken aback. Being a person of faith, I've heard that phrase many times, but not in a government building. This was a meeting called by a local government official and it was being held inside a government building. After the prayer, I turned to my friend Larry, who had invited me to the meeting and said, "That never would have happened in Maryland."

The meeting was about prison re-entry. Local church leaders of all faiths, people from the department of corrections, the local chamber of commerce, leaders of local charities, and a lot of other concerned citizens were there. Everyone seemed to know each other and be totally comfortable—it was apparent that these local leaders were all used to meeting together. Obviously, they also prayed together and actively worked to bring about good in the community.

Before Linda and I left Maryland, the 2015 Baltimore riots had broken out. A black man named Freddy Gray had died while in police custody. Six officers were involved. The medical examiner ruled it a homicide, but somehow three of the police officers involved were acquitted. After that, the state attorney dropped all charges against the remaining three officers. The Baltimore Police Department and other government officials seemed inept at best—purposely lying, obfuscating, and trying to cover their tracks at worst. The whole thing was horrible.

In my mind, I contrast this to events that occurred in Tuscaloosa shortly after we moved here. A black man from a local black community in Tuscaloosa county died while being arrested. Having just lived through Baltimore riots a few months prior, I immediately said to Linda, "Oh no. Here we go again."

I guess I expected another inept response from government. Obscure. Confuse. Hide. Deny.

Instead, what happened was amazing. Just like in the Freddy Gray case, the cause of death wasn't quite clear. No one was completely sure what had happened. Rumors swirled among the public that he had been shot, tazed, and beaten.[1] But instead of waiting, trying to buy time, and trying to keep certain details from becoming public, local government officials did the exact opposite.

They posted hours of recorded video, which was everything they had. Whatever information came in, they quickly released it to the public. They investigated. They probed. They seemed genuinely determined to get to the bottom of what happened, and genuinely concerned about healing and good relations with everyone in our communities. Community leaders of all faiths and races were in the inner circle of information. News updates were frequent and professional.

As it turned out, the young man had a large amount of cocaine, amphetamine, and alcohol in his system. He also had an enlarged heart and a thyroid condition. Sadly, he had died of a heart attack during the arrest and police had worked hard to try to save his life.[2]

Being friends with a local government official who was intimately involved in the investigation of these events, I asked about the handling of the matter, contrasting it to what we had seen in Baltimore. This person confirmed to me that the group of leaders who dealt with this crisis are the same group of leaders who meet on a regular basis to come up with proactive solutions for the community.

One of my favorite commercials right now is the one where the couple is standing outside looking at a burning building. The wife says, "Someone has burned down my she shed."

To which the husband replies, "Your she shed was struck by lightning, Cheryl."

My brain must go to strange places sometimes, because for whatever reason, this commercial makes me think that it was too late for Cheryl to practice fire prevention by installing lightning rods. This is also true for government. Once a problem is in motion, it's a little late to start preparing.

Communities must be connected to each other. If you are community leader, whether government or otherwise, actively work to connect your community. Band together. Work to solve problems. Here are a few other things I've observed from the local communities here:

(1) The local district attorney hosts community meetings to get all of the local charities together. The idea is to find out what synergies we can cultivate across the community, build unity, and work together to solve problems.

(2) The local chamber of commerce is very active, always putting on events of various kinds. Since most local businesses and non-profits are members, we all see each other on a routine basis. This creates a sense of connection and unity.

(3) All of the local law enforcement agencies participate in a lot of social and charity events in the community. And people from the community are actually involved too. It's not just a photo shoot for the media.

There are a lot of other examples of intentional cooperation between government, charities, churches, businesses, and higher education.

The main point here is that communities must be connected to themselves. While some of this may happen organically, it won't be nearly as effective unless a group of local leaders gets together and decides to be intentional about it. Cows don't stay milked. A lot of effort is required to maintain a spirit of unity and cooperation.

THIRTEEN

Affecting Change through Business

Sam used to run a filling machine at the paint factory in Chattanooga. He wore dark blue work pants, a light blue shirt with his name over the pocket, a white hard hat, and safety glasses. The safety glasses were something I mandated when I took over the plant, but Sam wore them well.

Pants and shirt always freshly pressed, it was clear Sam took an enormous amount of pride in himself and his work area. His work area was always pristine, which is not the norm for a paint factory. Sam always had a smile on his face. It was such a joy to talk to him that I never missed an opportunity. He and his wife raised seven children, all of which went on to graduate college.

Sam was one of about ten black men that worked at the facility who were also Korean War veterans. I tell the story about Sam because he and his family are a beautiful picture of upward mobility. Sam did not grow up with very much and neither did his wife. But they were able to provide a solid middle-class life for their children. And all seven graduating college—that would be an amazing track record in even the most privileged of families these days.

Manufacturing is the key to much of our success as a country. A wonderful friend of mine, the late Gus Whalen, once said there are three ways to generate wealth:

1. You can farm it.
2. You can mine it.
3. You can make it.

The highest value add is in the making it. Governments desperately need to understand the importance of manufacturing. If they truly understand, they will do whatever they can to keep and expand our manufacturing base.

Manufacturing provides good jobs to the lower and lower-middle class. They provide an excellent means of upward mobility, which is critical for everyone, and especially minorities.

Large manufacturing companies provide benefits to their employees that aren't available elsewhere. Savings plans, health care, and tons of scholarships, training, and other opportunities for education. Many of them reach out into marginalized communities to help.

In my view, business is probably one of the most advanced arenas with regard to addressing racism and injustice. Larger companies especially tend to go out of their way to address these problems.

Bottom line, I think working toward expanding our manufacturing base will actually do a lot to improve race relations and correct injustice in this country. What ideas do you have for increasing racial harmony through the business world?

FOURTEEN

The Impact of Higher Education

For the people who choose to go, college is one of the most impactful times of their life. Learning new things is important but meeting new people and establishing new networks are equally important. Often, these last for a lifetime. Anyone who is involved in higher education has an awesome responsibility—and an opportunity to do good in the world.

The types of colleges and universities that exist are very diverse, ranging from military academies, liberal arts colleges, seminaries, traditionally black colleges, private colleges, and large state universities. However, a calculus class at the local community college teaches the same material as a calculus class at Harvard. Often they may even use the same textbooks.

Besides academic competition and rigor, what really differentiates colleges is their out of classroom experience and the network experience an alumnus has after graduation. The academics were basically the same at the

University of Alabama as they were at the Naval Academy—chemistry does not change when you move south. But my out of classroom experiences at the two were vastly different.

The point is that out of classroom experiences are the area where colleges and universities can have the most impact to drive better race relations. Instead of designing more diversity curriculums, those in higher education should be thinking about how to bring students of different races together outside of the classroom.

What Gets Measured and Tracked Gets Attention

If something is important, then it should be measured and monitored. Recently, the College of Engineering at the University of Alabama experienced a decrease in the percentage of black students enrolled. There were simultaneously experiencing a drop in the percentage of black students that were graduating.

Enrollment in the college was growing, but the overall number of black students stayed flat. This caused concern so a focus group was formed. Various alumni and academics came together to address the issue. One of the recommendations was to hire a full-time staff member to work solely on this issue. The two major concerns were, of course, recruitment and retention.

Regarding recruitment, the college identified the top twenty high schools in the state that would have significant numbers of black students who meet the requirements for admission. The dean, influential students, and alumni associated with the college visited those schools. They mingled with high achieving candidates and spoke to the student bodies about the benefits of an engineering degree. They also shared about their experiences at the university.

The big key here is intentionality. The college was intentional about increasing the number of black students.

The next part of the effort involved increasing retention. Retention requires an organizational culture where students feel welcomed, accepted, and that they are a meaningful part of the organization. Many out of classroom activities help with this.

For example, the UA College of Engineering is currently forming an honors social justice student organization. The idea is for engineers to use their skills to make a difference in the lives of those less fortunate. For example, clean water is an issue in rural parts of the US and in developing countries. Getting students involved in those types of programs can be life-changing for them.

Tutoring programs, co-op programs, engineering competitions, and other such programs are other great ways to actively get black students involved in student life. These types of activities are chances for students to learn, have fun, and get to know each other.

We have to be intentional about making sure that minority students are invited, recruited, and included in these types of activities.

Another organization I'm involved with at UA is the

Blackburn Institute. I'm fortunate to serve on the advisory board. The Blackburn Institute was formed to develop leaders for the state of Alabama. For students, being accepted into the institute is highly competitive. It's quite an honor for them to be involved, and it's also a lot of work.

The Blackburn Institute tracks the racial, gender, and regional makeup of the students in the program. We are intentionally diverse, so the program benefits young black leaders in several ways. There are benefits to their personal and leadership development, as well as networking opportunities.

The idea here is that if you are an alumnus, teacher, or staff member for a college, you can take what you are passionate about and turn it into a venue for helping people of other races—even if the purpose doesn't primarily revolve around race. You can also form many friendships with people of other races this way. Many of the young black men that contributed to this book are friends that I met through the Blackburn Institute.

Greek Systems

A major part of the out of classroom experience, especially in the south, is the Greek system. When I was in school there were white fraternities and sororities, black fraternities and sororities, and Jewish fraternities and sororities. Initially my perception was that today the formerly white fraternities are integrated but the historically black fraternities are not. I was wrong about that, at least partially.

Almost all of the young black men I consulted about this book are members of a mostly or all-black fraternities, so I asked them to speak to that issue. Here are some snippets of what I heard:

- *Our black fraternities are elite groups. It is a collection of men that are educated and have the same values. As far as the type of person they wanted to have as a fraternity brother, it is not unlike what we would expect to hear from any other fraternity.*

- *Each black fraternity involves a lifetime commitment of service to black communities.*

- *Our black fraternity has been integrated since 1945. We welcome people from other races.*

- *The white fraternity "integration" probably means 7 black guys and 150 white guys. The perception [among many black people] is that it requires a lot of money to be a member.*

There was a lot of difference between what the most recent graduates expressed verses the ones that graduated ten or more years ago. Most of the recent grads portrayed a Greek system that was working toward diversity. They indicated that the fraternities intermingled productively among one another. I left the discussion feeling encouraged that both blacks and whites were making an effort.

Still, there is an end goal and we aren't there yet. Most universities still have a long way to go toward fully integrating their Greek systems. No organization should be allowed to deny membership solely based on race. However, it could prove quite problematic to give Greek organizations a race quota. Maybe a staggered quota that achieves full representation of minorities over time would be a good approach. The issue should definitely be studied at universities which have an integration issue in their Greek systems.

In the meantime, black and white Greek organizations can join together for entertainment or service projects. There are certainly innovative ways to foster relationships between black and white fraternities and sororities.

Leveraging the Existing Unity of Alumi

Another area where colleges and universities can make progress is to leverage the built-in unity that exists among alumni. The example Alex Smith shared in the Foreword to this book was a good example of an alumni association taking a practical step. In addition to alumni associations, there are ample opportunities to get alumni involved with department advisory boards, co-op programs, internships, student visits to businesses, mentorships, and class speakers.

A major key to racial harmony is getting people united around a common goal. If I go to the grocery store and see a black family decked out in University of Alabama sweatshirts, I have an immediate bond with them. We could all use a starting point of some kind.

Universities supporting regional alumni groups could encourage them to be intentional about building friendships with people of other races. They are already unified to some degree around their common school experience, so that is a good starting point.

Being intentional, as always, is the key. Colleges and universities have the potential to make a great impact in this area. Let's seize the opportunity together!

FIFTEEN

Let's Go Change the World

When I felt God prodding me to address this issue, I suspected he was doing the same thing with a lot of other people. Either way, I feel very confident in saying that God intends for all of us in America to get with the program and fix the problem of racial injustice. To accomplish this, he will probably use a lot of different messengers coming from a lot of different angles—men and women of all races and backgrounds.

For the most part, we have a stronger tendency to listen to people that we have a lot in common with. I'm white, a veteran, and an engineer. I'm Christian, a small business owner, and I have background in manufacturing. So I can probably reach a good number of people with similar backgrounds.

At the same time, we must commit ourselves to listen to and learn from people of different backgrounds. They are the ones who can teach us the most. For instance, my friend, Gaston Large, offered up this perspective:

> *"Have you ever gone to a meeting where you were the only one in a suit? Or you're wearing a red shirt and everyone else is wearing blue? It would probably feel a little uncomfortable. So imagine growing up most of your life that way. It can be uncomfortable at times."*

We just don't have that experience. So the only way to learn about it is by listening to someone who does have that experience. That's where we start. We start by listening to others with open hearts and minds.

Then we take what we've learned and we apply it to our own hearts. Culture change starts within each individual. We need to honor each other. We need to see the image of God in each person. We need unity among people of all races. We need brotherly love for each other. We need to be humble and tender-hearted. We need to speak life and blessing over each other.

God can do all of those things in and through us if we ask him. Only he can change what's in our hearts. As we ask him to do what only he can do, we must go out and do everything we can do. The heart change will come through prayer that is followed up by action.

Earlier in the book, I mentioned figuring out what we could personally do to help in our spheres of influence. Just meeting with friends or working within the PTA, little league, or in social circles.

But some of you are actually capable of more than this. Some of you are capable of a lot more. You're naturally gifted at communicating and networking. You're a gifted leader. You know people of influence and authority, and you're good at getting things done. Some of you have your mayors and police chiefs and sheriffs on speed dial.

I'd like to encourage you to figure out what you can personally do to raise awareness and drive change, especially on the issue of police treatment of black people. That is undoubtedly the number one issue facing us today. We can all work to drive more fairness and equity in our workplaces and other organizations, and do a lot of other things to help.

But there's nothing more basic, foundational, and gravely serious than a group of people being unfairly targeted by police. The worst part of all this is that the police are actually supposed to be there to protect us. Can you imagine what it would be like to be afraid of the police? Can you imagine never calling the police—even if you were the victim of a crime—because you're scared they would somehow turn the situation around and use it against you? Can you imagine being afraid to call the police because you're concerned that they would show up on the scene and mistake you for the criminal?

This is the major issue of our day.

While it might be more than I can personally pull together at my age, I would encourage someone to study in depth the issue of what leads to police violence, especially on minorities.

I suspect there is a lot we can do in terms of developing how officers are selected and trained. My hunch is that a good starting point would be testing the EQ (emotional intelligence) of officers.

Being someone with expertise in the area of EQ, personality profiles, and personal strengths and weaknesses, I would be interested in studying this area. But I do not have the law enforcement background and connection. So if anyone out there reading does have those things, or some kind of relevant expertise, and you're interested in putting our heads together to try to solve this problem, I am game. Let's do it!

Whatever actions have come to mind for you while reading this book, the key is to choose one or two or three of them and go do it! Start now. If you wait, you're likely to forget much of what you've thought about, felt, and prayed for during this time. But if you pick up the phone right now, you just might set into motion a series of events that will change the world.

Go and change the world.

God is with you.

CALLED WRITERS
CHRISTIAN PUBLISHING

Please visit **CalledWriters.com** for articles, videos, and other resources by Christian authors and ministers!

We are a relatively new Christian publishing house, dedicated to bringing you authors who are divinely gifted, anointed, and called by God for such a time as this.

We would love to connect with you on social media as well:

Facebook.com/CalledWriters

Twitter: @CalledWriters

Instagram: @CalledWriters

The Jericho Fast: How to Break through Walls with Prayer and Fasting

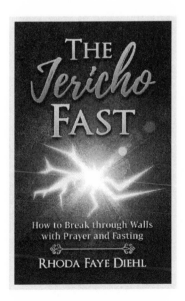

Available on Amazon

Speaking in Tongues: Enjoying Intimacy With God
Through Tongues and Interpretation

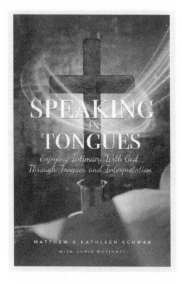

Available on Amazon

References and Notes

3. The Washington Redskins

1. John Keim, "Redskins removing name of former owner George Preston Marshall from Ring of Fame," espn.com, ESPN, Jun 24, 2020, https://www.espn.com/nfl/story/_/id/29358399/source-redskins-removing-name-former-owner-george-preston-marshall-ring-fame.
2. Thomas G. Smith, "1962: The Year That Changed the Redskins," washingtonian.com, Washingtonian, October 10, 2011, https://www.washingtonian.com/2011/10/10/1962-the-year-that-changed-the-redskins/.

5. The United States Naval Academy

1. "Proverbs 19:18," biblehub.com, Bible Hub, August 19, 2020, https://biblehub.com/proverbs/19-18.htm

9. What Can Us White Guys Do to Make Things Better?

1. Christopher Klein, "Teen Debunks Professor's Claim That Anti-Irish Signs Never Existed," history.com, History, August 22, 2018, https://www.history.com/news/teen-debunks-professors-claim-that-anti-irish-signs-never-existed
2. Matthew Brown, "Fact check: The Irish were Indentured servants, not slaves," usatoday.com, USA Today, June 18, 2020, https://www.usatoday.com/story/news/factcheck/2020/06/18/fact-check-irish-were-indentured-servants-not-slaves/3198590001/
3. Mona Chalabi, "Dear Mona, How Many Kids Have Trust Funds?," fivethirtyeight.com, FiveThirtyEight, August 21, 2014,

https://fivethirtyeight.com/features/dear-mona-how-many-kids-have-trust-funds/

4. Amy Fontinelle, "Why millennials should not rely on an inheritance," blog.massmutual.com, MassMutual, July 28, 2020, https://blog.massmutual.com/post/why-millennials-should-not-rely-on-an-inheritance

5. Chris Hogan, "How Many Millionaires Actually Inherited Their Wealth?," chrishogan360.com, Chris Hogan, August 19, 2020, https://www.chrishogan360.com/investing/how-many-millionaires-actually-inherited-their-wealth

6. Amy Fontinelle, "Why millennials should not rely on an inheritance," blog.massmutual.com, MassMutual, July 28, 2020, https://blog.massmutual.com/post/why-millennials-should-not-rely-on-an-inheritance

7. I am only referring to general use of the phrase and message that "Black lives matter." I am not endorsing or promoting the organization which has adopted that name as the name for their organization. Readers would have to research that organization and draw their own conclusions.

8. Lucado, Max. *Grace for the Moment.* J. Countryman, 2000.

9. Extensive studies would have to be done to know whether this is actually the case on a wider scale. Determining which part of the country has the best racial integration is not my primary goal here. I'm just relaying what we have personally experienced and observed. The primary point is that racial integration of neighborhoods and organizations matters. It's hard to love and appreciate people from a distance.

10. Try Not to Do Anything Stupid

1. Tyler Martin, "Alabama Assistant Coach Apologizes After Former Gymnast Accuses Him Of Racist Language," si.com, SI, June 3, 2020, https://www.si.com/college/alabama/bamacentral/former-ua-gymnast-tia-kiaku-alleges-assistant-coach-of-using-racially-charged-language

2. Erik Evans, "Duckworth's Non-Apology Comes Up Woefully Short," rollbamaroll.com, SB Nation, June 5, 2020, https://www.rollbamaroll.com/2020/6/5/21281428/read-the-room-duckworths-non-apology-comes-up-woefully-short

3. Sean Prince, "Straight Talk About the N-Word," tolerance.org, Teaching Tolerance, Fall 2011, https://www.tolerance.org/magazine/fall-2011/straight-talk-about-the-nword

12. Being Active in Government

1. Stephanie Taylor, "Tuscaloosa Police release video from night man died during arrest," tuscaloosanews.com, Tuscaloosa News, July 15, 2015, https://www.tuscaloosanews.com/article/DA/20150715/News/605153985/TL
2. Stephanie Taylor, "DA says Ware died of drug toxicity," tuscaloosanews.com, Tuscaloosa News, August 26, 2015, https://www.tuscaloosanews.com/article/DA/20150826/News/605155458/TL

About the Author

John Covington has been married to his lovely wife, Linda, since 1972. John is the founder and CEO of Chesapeake Consulting. He attended the United States Naval Academy and the University of Alabama earning a degree in chemical engineering. He is a distinguished fellow of both The University of Alabama College of Engineering and the Department of Chemical and Biological Engineering. Prior to starting Chesapeake Consulting, he served industry in a variety of positions including engineer, plant manager, and vice president of operations. He is an active member of Church of the Highlands in Tuscaloosa, Alabama, and volunteers with prison re-entry efforts and prison ministry. In his spare time, he enjoys playing with his German Shepherd, Willow, and helping others train their dogs. This is John's seventh book on leadership and faith.